MILADY'S STANDARD
Nail Technology
Student Workbook

6th Edition

By Alisha Rimando Botero

Revised by Catherine Frangie

Australia • Brazil • Japan • Korea • Mexico • Singapore • Spain • United Kingdom • United States

Milady's Standard: Nail Technology Student Workbook, Sixth edition
Author(s): Alisha Rimando Botero
Contributor: Catherine Frangie

President, Milady: Dawn Gerrain

Publisher: Erin O'Connor

Acquisitions Editor: Martine Edwards

Product Manager: Jessica Mahoney

Editorial Assistant: Elizabeth A. Edwards

Director of Beauty Industry Relations:
   Sandra Bruce

Senior Marketing Manager: Gerard McAvey

Production Director: Wendy Troeger

Senior Content Project Manager:
   Nina Tucciarelli

Senior Art Director: Joy Kocsis

For product information and technology assistance, contact us at
Cengage Learning Customer & Sales Support, 1-800-354-9706

For permission to use material from this text or product,
submit all requests online at **www.cengage.com/permissions**
Further permissions questions can be emailed to
permissionrequest@cengage.com

Library of Congress Control Number: 2007941007

ISBN-13: 978-1-4354-9764-1

ISBN-10: 1-4354-9764-3

Milady
Executive Woods
5 Maxwell Drive
Clifton Park, NY 12065
USA

Cengage Learning is a leading provider of customized learning solutions with office locations around the globe, including Singapore, the United Kingdom, Australia, Mexico, Brazil, and Japan. Locate your local office at **www.cengage.com/global**

Cengage Learning products are represented in Canada by Nelson Education, Ltd.

To learn more about Milady, visit **milady.cengage.com**

Purchase any of our products at your local college store or at our preferred online store **www.cengagebrain.com**

Notice to the Reader

Publisher does not warrant or guarantee any of the products described herein or perform any independent analysis in connection with any of the product information contained herein. Publisher does not assume, and expressly disclaims, any obligation to obtain and include information other than that provided to it by the manufacturer. The reader is expressly warned to consider and adopt all safety precautions that might be indicated by the activities described herein and to avoid all potential hazards. By following the instructions contained herein, the reader willingly assumes all risks in connection with such instructions. The publisher makes no representations or warranties of any kind, including but not limited to, the warranties of fitness for particular purpose or merchantability, nor are any such representations implied with respect to the material set forth herein, and the publisher takes no responsibility with respect to such material. The publisher shall not be liable for any special, consequential, or exemplary damages resulting, in whole or part, from the readers' use of, or reliance upon, this material.

Printed in China
4 5 6 7 16 15 14 13 12

table of contents

About The Author

Alisha Rimando Botero is recognized as one of the nail industry's leading experts in training and education. Over the past 14 years in the professional beauty industry, Alisha's work has been described as "ground-breaking!" In this time she has been a platform artist and motivational speaker for more than 1,500 promotional and educational events, and has competed in over 100 nail competitions around the globe. Alisha was honored to win the World Championship in 2005.

Alisha has been the featured nail tech in dozens of training videos, and in more than 150 beauty and trade publications and blog spots world-wide; including *Teen Vogue Magazine, Bridal Guide Magazine, Self Magazine, Fitness Magazine* and *Seventeen Magazine*. Her work has been featured in and on the covers of numerous industry trade magazines such as *Nails Magazine, Nailpro Magazine, Scratch Magazine (UK)* and *Stylish Nail Magazine (Japan)*.

Throughout her career, Alisha has garnered the attention of large industry manufacturers, small business entrepreneurs, salon franchises, and nail and beauty associations. She has worked with R&D chemists to develop a myriad of nail enhancement products, nanotechnology skin care and cuticle treatments, polish collections, and natural nail treatments. Several products and lines she has had a hand in creating and marketing have been recognized with READERS' CHOICE AWARDS for best products and one being the recipient of the coveted ABBIE award for best packaging.

Alisha's flawless nail creations have been sought after and used in numerous ads and campaigns where hands and feet play a pivotal role for product sales. She continues to achieve notoriety as "manicurist to the stars", and recently was featured with Jennifer Hudson in her video "Spotlight."

Alisha has worked with designers Isaac Mizrahi, Diane von Furstenberg, Zac Posen, Tony Cohen, and many others during various NYC Fashion Weeks, creating innovative nail looks for their runway shows.

Alisha is also a prominent and well-known educator, teaching nail classes in over a hundred beauty schools and vocational schools across the US. On the international front, she is also responsible for implementing artistic training programs and marketing strategies that resulted in the opening of over 100 nail salons and 7 schools in Japan, growing that market to become the industry leader in nail art techniques.

Ever-growing and changing, Alisha's career took her into the publishing world when she was asked to be a contributing author to both *Milady's Standard Nail Technology* and *Milady's Standard Cosmetology* textbooks.

Recognizing her talent and commitment to education, Milady also engaged her to author *Milady's Standard Nail Technology Workbook*.

Alisha's love and passion for her industry and her family have led her to New York where she currently resides with her husband and son.

Special Thanks

To my husband, Rodrigo Botero, you are the butter to my bread, the breath to my life, only with your support and guidance was this possible.

To my mother, Karen Gainey, for being my rock throughout my career and life.

To my son, Aspen Rodeck Botero, for all the much needed interruptions while writing—you are my heart, my muse, my everything!

To Tom Holcomb, my partner in this ever-changing industry, my friend, and my mentor. This was possible because of your love and care in my development as an artist and a person.

And finally, to Cathy Frangie, for believing in me and guiding me down a new path in my life. I am forever grateful.

Introduction

Welcome to an exciting career in nail technology!

This workbook is intended for use with your textbook and to assist you in remembering all the important information you will use in your career as a nail technician! In addition to helping you to review and learn all of the material in your textbook, this workbook also includes the information you will need to prepare for and take your state's licensing exam.

For the first time ever, *Milady's Standard Nail Technology Workbook* was designed and created to challenge and stimulate you! Nail technology students will be prompted to think about their nail careers and the principles that are taught in *Milady's Standard Nail Technology* textbook and to answer thought-provoking and intriguing questions.

As you delve into this workbook, you will find pages filled with challenging puzzles, fun facts, interesting salon scenarios, and hands-on practice exercises that will help you to master the techniques a nail technician will use everyday in the salon.

As you read through the workbook remember to use your *Milady's Standard Nail Technology* textbook as a reference point for finding information. By the time you are finished with this workbook, you will be well on your way to passing your licensing exam and having a fun and exciting career in nail technology!

Part 1

ORIENTATION

1
history and
opportunities

Welcome! You have made one of the greatest decisions you have made in your life so far—to begin a career in nail technology!

We are now going to review the history and opportunities of this exciting career.

Key Terms

in your own words

Describe the difference between cosmetology and nail technology.

_____

_____

_____

_____

_____

_____

_____

_____

A Brief History of Cosmetology and Nail Technology

the origins of self-beautification

Using the words provided, fill in the blanks below to complete these statements about the origins of self-beautification.

beauty	Dead Sea	henna	natural
beeswax	egg whites	herbs	nuts
berries	Egypt	hide	oil
bit	essential oils	insects	oyster shells
black	flints	leaves	pinched
blonde	gelatin	leisure	red
bone	Greek	long nails	Roman Empire
chamois cloth	gum arabic	manicured	roots
class status	hairstyling	masks	tree bark
Cosmetics	health	minerals	wealth

1. Grooming implements used at the dawn of history were shaped from sharpened

   _____, _____, or _____.

2. Strips of animal _____ were used to tie back the hair.

3. Natural elements were used to create pigments for coloring the hair, skin, and nails. These pigments were made from _____, _____,

   _____, _____, _____,

   _____, _____, _____, and

   other materials.

4. Egyptians used _____ to stain their hair and nails a rich, warm red in as early as 3000 B.C.

5. In both ancient _____ and the _____, military commanders stained their nails and lips in matching colors before important battles. Later, _____ soldiers also did this when preparing for battle.

6. Queen Nefertiti used custom-blended _____ as signature scents in 1400 BC.

7. Queen Cleopatra erected a personal (cosmetics) factory next to the _____ in 50 BC.

8. Chinese aristocrats rubbed a tinted mixture of_____, _____, _____, and _____ onto their nails to turn them crimson or ebony in 1600 BC.

9. Extraordinarily_____ represented _____ and _____ and were status symbols of the ancient Chinese elite.

10. _____ became a highly developed art during the Golden Age of Greece.

11. Roman women used hair color to indicate their _____ Noblewomen colored their hair _____, middle-class women colored their hair _____, and poor women colored their hair _____.

12. During the Renaissance period people of wealth _____ their nails, as evidenced by archeological digs.

13. During the reign of Queen Victoria of England, women wanted to preserve the _____ and _____ of their skin, so they used beauty _____ and packs made from honey, eggs, milk, oatmeal, fruits, vegetables, and other natural ingredients.

14. Victorian women would sometimes tint their nails with red _____ and then buffed with a _____.

15. Victorian women _____ their cheeks and _____ their lips to induce _____ color.

© MILADY, A PART OF CENGAGE LEARNING.

Career Paths For a Nail Technician

working as a nail technician

In the table below list the benefits of working as a nail technician in each of the different environments listed.

Working Environments for a Nail Technician			
NAIL SALON	FULL-SERVICE SALON	DAY SPA	MEDICAL SPA

in your own words

Review your answers in the table above. In the space provided below, explain which setting fits your personality and long-term goals best. Why?

a bright future

List the additional career opportunities for a licensed nail technician mentioned in Chapter 1 that **do not** involve building a clientele behind the nail table.

- _____
- _____
- _____
- _____
- _____
- _____
- _____
- _____
- _____
- _____
- _____
- _____
- _____
- _____

chapter 1: history review

Complete the statements below about nail technology advancements since the twentieth century by circling the correct answer.

© HANA, 2010. USED UNDER LICENSE FROM SHUTTERSTOCK.COM

1. With the invention of motion pictures, what standards of feminine beauty began to change?
   a. Flawless complexions
   b. Beautiful hairstyles
   c. Manicured nails
   d. All of the above

2. Who began manufacturing and selling makeup to movie stars that wouldn't cake or crack, even under hot studio lights?
   a. Max Factor
   b. Charles Revson
   c. Jeff Pink
   d. Jean Harlow

3. What company introduced the first emery board in 1910 that is nearly identical to the emery boards used today?
   a. Graf's Hyglo
   b. Flowery Manicure Products
   c. Revlon
   d. Max Factor

4. Who introduced the first mass-market nail lacquers in a variety of colors?
   a. Max Factor
   b. Charles Revson
   c. Jeff Pink
   d. Flowery Manicure Products

5. What type of manicure was considered the ultimate luxury in nail and hand care in the 1950s?
   a. Spa manicures
   b. Hot oil manicures
   c. French manicures
   d. None of the above

6. What type of nail wraps were commonly used to protect natural nail tips in the 1960s?
   a. Fiberglass wraps
   b. Silk wraps
   c. Juliette paper wraps
   d. Plastic wraps

7. Who invented ridge filler and the French manicure?
   a. Max Factor
   b. Charles Revson
   c. Jeff Pink
   d. Flowery Manicure Products

8. In what decade were the first monomer liquid and polymer powder nail services offered by nail technicians?
   a. 1950s
   b. 1960s
   c. 1970s
   d. 1980s

9. When was nail grooming no longer considered a luxury, but expected as part of every client's grooming ritual?
   a. Victorian Age
   b. Renaissance Age
   c. Twentieth century
   d. Twenty-first century

10. In the twenty-first century, what nail product formulations improved dramatically?
    a. UV gels
    b. Polish formulations
    c. Foot and hand skin treatments
    d. All of the above

2 life skills

Hey, this section is all about you—building your life and career skills! Here, we will review techniques to manage your career—from adapting to new study skills to working each day to keep a positive attitude—the skills discussed in this chapter will help you succeed in your new profession and in your life! So, pay attention!

life skills crossword puzzle

Fill in the crossword puzzle by using the clues below.

ACROSS

4 To make a list of tasks that need to be done in the order of most important to least important.

7 A statement that establishes the values that a business or an individual lives by and that sets up future goals.

DOWN

1 Putting off until tomorrow what you can do today.

2 An unhealthy compulsion to do things perfectly.

3 Identifying short-term and long-term goals to help you decide what you want to achieve in your life.

5 Principles of good character, proper conduct, and moral judgment, expressed through personality, human relation skills, and professional image.

6 The conscious act of planning your life rather than just letting things happen.

The Psychology of Success

guidelines to success double puzzle

Unscramble the principles that contribute to personal and professional success listed below and write the phrase inside the cells. Copy the letters in the numbered cells to the other cells with the same number to reveal the secret message!

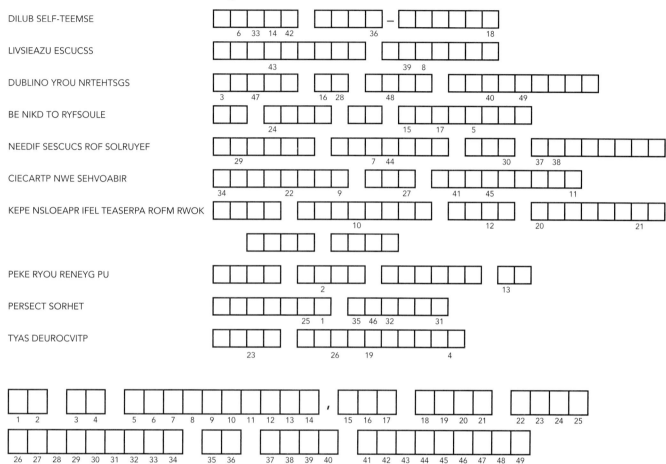

DILUB SELF-TEEMSE

LIVSIEAZU ESCUCSS

DUBLINO YROU NRTEHTSGS

BE NIKD TO RYFSOULE

NEEDIF SESCUCS ROF SOLRUYEF

CIECARTP NWE SEHVOABIR

KEPE NSLOEAPR IFEL TEASERPA ROFM RWOK

PEKE RYOU RENEYG PU

PERSECT SORHET

TYAS DEUROCVITP

Managing Your Career

in your own words

Create a mission statement, and be sure it communicates who you are and what you want out of life.

Now that you have your mission statement, use the space below to set at least 3 short-term and long-term goals. Remember that by mapping out your goals, you will see where you need to focus your attention, and what you need to learn in order to fulfill your dreams.

Short term goals to complete this year (be realistic!):

1. _____

2. _____

3. _____

Long term goals to achieve in the next 5-10 years (shoot for the stars!):

1. _____

2. _____

3. _____

Tech **Tip:**

> When setting goals it's important to have a plan and re-examine it often to make sure that you are staying on track. Keep the goals and your plan somewhere that is easily visible to you everyday— keeping your goals on the top of your mind is a great first step to accomplishing them!

time management

Answer true or false to the following expert tips on making time more manageable.

T   F   **1.** You can learn to prioritize by making a list of tasks that need to be done in order from most important to least important.

T   F   **2.** You will find it easier to complete your tasks if you limit your activities and don't spread yourself too thin.

T   F   **3.** When designing your own time management system, make sure to schedule in some time for checking your email.

T   F   **4.** Plan your daily, weekly, and monthly schedules around your leisure time as it's important to get enough time for yourself.

T   F   **5.** Carry a notepad or an organizer with you at all times to record ideas before they slip your mind!

T F **6.** Buy yourself something whenever you are frustrated, overwhelmed, worried, or feeling guilty about something.

T F **7.** Exercise and recreation stimulate clear thinking and planning, so do not neglect physical activity.

T F **8.** Reward yourself with a special treat or activity for work well done and time managed efficiently.

T F **9.** The key to organizing your time efficiently is to procrastinate when it's time for tasks and activities you don't really want to do.

T F **10.** Make time management a habit.

study skills

EFFORT + FOLLOW THROUGH = SUCCESSFUL CAREER

Don't worry, the equation above isn't really math—it's a way to remember that every effort you make to follow through on your education is an investment in your future. In the space below explain where, when, and how you will study using the good study habits you learned from Chapter 2.

Where? Describe your environment.

_____

_____

_____

_____

When? Describe when is the best time for you to study.

_____

_____

_____

_____

How? Describe how you will retain the information you are studying.

_____

_____

_____

_____

Personality Development and Attitude

your healthy positive attitude

Match these characteristics of a healthy, positive attitude with their descriptions.

_____ 1. Communication skills

_____ 2. Receptivity

_____ 3. Emotional stability

_____ 4. Diplomacy

_____ 5. Values and goals

_____ 6. Self Care

_____ 7. Tone of voice

_____ 8. Sensitivity

A. Learning how to handle a confrontation, as well as sharing how you feel without going overboard, are important indicators of maturity.

B. Being compassionate and responsive to other people.

C. These show us how to behave, and what to aim toward.

D. To be interested in other people, and to be responsive to their opinions, feelings, and ideas.

E. Talking about yourself and listening to what others have to say, and when you want something, asking for it clearly and directly.

F. If you have a positive attitude, you can deliver your words more pleasantly.

G. Being tactful means being straightforward, not critical.

H. If you are to be truly helpful to others, it is essential to take care of yourself.

Fun **Fact...**

Having a game plan is the conscious act of planning your life, rather than just letting things happen. While an overall game plan is usually organized into large blocks of time, such as five or ten years, it is just as important to set daily, monthly, and yearly goals.

chapter 2: life skills review

Complete the multiple-choice questions below by circling the correct answer to each question.

1. If motivation propels you to do something, then self-management is:
   a. The ever changing world
   b. A well-thought-out process for the long haul
   c. An external push
   d. None of the above

2. How can you enhance your creativity?
   a. Do not be self-critical.
   b. Be alone.
   c. Build a positive vocabulary.
   d. A and C

3. If you pay attention to _____, you can learn how to manage your time most efficiently and reach your goals faster.
   a. Your mission statement
   b. Your inner voice
   c. Your natural rhythms
   d. Your mother

4. What are ethics?
   a. Principles of good character
   b. Improper conduct
   c. Judgment of others
   d. B and C

5. How are ethics expressed?
   a. Through personality
   b. Through human relations skills
   c. Through professional image
   d. All of the above

6. What will increase as you make progress with your learning?
   a. Confidence and self-esteem
   b. Time management skills
   c. Good study habits
   d. Brain capacity

7. How can you become more comfortable and successful at learning new material?
   a. Study the new material alone
   b. Write down key words or phrases as your instructor discusses them
   c. Study in larger chunks of time
   d. B and C

8. Which is an example of a short-term goal?
   a. Own your own salon.
   b. Buy your dream home.
   c. Pass your next theory exam.
   d. None of the above.

9. Which is an example of a long-term goal?
   a. Own your own salon.
   b. Buy your dream home.
   c. Graduate nail school.
   d. A and B.

10. What does a mission statement do?
    a. Point you in a solid direction
    b. Help manage your career
    c. Help in creating short and long term goals
    d. All of the above.

3

your
professional
image

As in all things in life, it's not just what you do but **how** you do it that counts the most—and your professional image is no exception! In this chapter we will review how to look, stand, and sit to convey a confident, professional image, as well as how to avoid physical injuries while practicing your craft in your new profession.

your professional image word scramble

Unscramble the key terms below and write the term on the line provided using the definitions shown.

ceosginrom

estsrs

onrsplea ehgnyie

plisyhac nreistoaenpt

poaofsenlrsi aegim

_____ Person's physical posture, walk, and movements.

_____ Impression projected by a person engaged in any profession, consisting of outward appearance and conduct exhibited in the workplace.

_____ Study of how a workplace and tools should be designed for maximum comfort, safety, efficiency, and productivity.

_____ A force or system of forces exerted on the body that result in strain and/or injury.

_____ Daily maintenance of cleanliness by practicing good sanitary habits.

Beauty and Wellness

personal and professional hygiene puzzle

It seems basic, but your professional hygiene is so important to your confidence and your client's ease and comfort with you. Let's have a little fun—fill in the blanks below to answer the questions about personal and professional hygiene. Then find those words in the word find puzzle on the following page.

1. One of the best ways to ensure that you always smell fresh and clean is to create a hygiene pack to keep in your station or locker. What eight products should your hygiene pack include?

   a. _____

   b. _____

   c. _____

   d. _____

   e. _____

   f. _____

   g. _____

   h. _____

2. If you smoke cigarettes during work hours, you should do what three things before servicing a client? (Note: One has been provided for you.)

a. _____

b. _____

c. use mouthwash _____

3. Being well _____ begins with _____ and

_____ fresh.

```
H E Q A R E A W X B B S S Y N V Z S R R
D D T V N B H R I R L M K R V W V W D E
G E N S F T P F E M G E J Y V Y C E S Z
N P M M A G I A E T N L V G P J L D Y I
I O M O Q P T P O V X L Q R I T K X S T
K I X K O H H O E M B I L A I M T S B I
O J E V M R T T E R H N M X O H O Y X N
O R C I H H G Q O J S G O U Z L T U N A
L Q N M B U D C J O P P T H F B G Q G S
E T N R P O W R P L T H I L A H T Z K D
S B U Z E S Z Y L P W C A R I H E G L N
L S O E X P S V P A O T U Z A D F J A A
H E C B A F D O S B N U M P X N N V N H
S R T T F A O H U E V W C K P C T B V S
Y J P Q Q X I Q D B R U S H T E E T H K
N W T N A R O D O E D S D N A H H S A W
C W C V N G D X M P M E E J B Y Q Z J E
Z D Q G D T V U J V K T U X N W F H O J
F C U R M E J R H H N E O T W I Q B J S
X B C L E E N N O T V J O D X A K I Y Y
```

Looking Good

dress for success

Answer true or false to the statements below about how you should dress at your place for employment.

T F **1.** Since you are in the beauty industry you can wear something wild and crazy like you would on the weekend.

T F **2.** Your professional image should be consistent with the image of the salon.

T F **3.** A professional image consists of outward appearance and conduct exhibited in the work-place.

T F **4.** Your clothing should not reflect the fashions of the season, and should remain a consis-tent uniform throughout the year.

T F **5.** Wear shoes that are fashionable, have a high heel, and make your legs look long.

T F **6.** Ensure your clothing is clean, fresh, and in step with fashion.

T F **7.** Accessorize your outfits, but make sure that your jewelry does not clank and jingle while working.

T F **8.** A clean, freshly scrubbed face is a beautiful and natural look, perfect for your professional image at the salon.

T F **9.** Let the salon's image be your guide on the right makeup choices to wear for work.

T F **10.** Choose clothing that is functional, as well as stylish.

© MILADY, A PART OF CENGAGE LEARNING. PHOTOGRAPHY BY PAUL CASTLE.

Fun **Fact...**

When you display good physical posture in your stance, walk and movements, it shows off your figure to its best advantage and conveys an image of confidence. So, remember this when walking into your next party or interview. You never get a second chance to make a first impression!

Your Physical Presentation

ergonomically correct postures and movements

Fill in the blank to complete the sentences below about how to create good posture and avoid injury and strain.

1. Good posture is a very important part of your physical presentation. Name the five ways you can practice good posture at work:

   a. Keep your neck _____ and _____ directly above the _____.

   b. Lift your _____ so that your _____ is out and up.

   c. Hold your shoulders _____ and _____.

   d. Sit with your back _____.

   e. Pull in your _____.

2. Each year, hundreds of nail technicians develop carpal tunnel syndrome and back injuries. These injuries are called _____.

3. An awareness of your body _____ and _____, coupled with better work habits and proper tools and equipment will enhance your _____ and _____.

4. Stressful repetitive motions have a _____ effect on the muscles and joints.

5. Describe the ways that you can prevent repetitive motion injuries:

   a. Use _____ designed implements.

   b. Never _____ or _____ implements too tightly.

   c. Avoid constantly _____ the wrist when using manicuring tools.

   d. Make sure that your _____ are never more than _____ away from your body for extended periods of time.

   e. Never _____ to get closer to your clients. Ask them to _____ their arms or legs _____ to you.

chapter 3: your professional image

Complete the multiple-choice questions below by circling the correct answer to each question.

1. Why do many salons have a no-fragrance policy for staff members during work hours?
   a. A significant number of people are sensitive or allergic to a variety of chemicals.
   b. Clients may only like the smell of particular fragrances.
   c. Salons frequently use aromatherapy and perfume interferes.
   d. Your perfume may offend customers.

2. What should you do as an advertisement for your commitment to professional beauty?
   a. Put thought into your appearance every day.
   b. Keep your haircut and color in tip-top shape.
   c. Determine the best length and grooming for your nails and meticulously maintain their appearance.
   d. All of the above

3. Each year, hundreds of cosmetology professionals report which musculoskeletal disorders?
   a. Carpal tunnel syndrome
   b. Tennis elbow
   c. Back injuries
   d. A and C

4. What is an example of ergonomic equipment?
   a. A stationary lamp
   b. Handicapped bathroom
   c. Handles or pulls on all drawers and cabinets
   d. A stool that can be raised and lowered

5. What should rule when it comes to choosing clothes to wear at work?
   a. Fashion
   b. Season
   c. Common sense
   d. Comfort

what would you do? a salon **scenario**

Your favorite client's daughter, Alessia, is coming in for her eighth birthday. She is scheduled for a little princess manicure with nail art on every finger. As she gets comfortable in the chair, you realize she is so small that you will have to lean in and bend forward throughout the entire one-hour service in order to reach her hands. What would you do to create a more ergonomically correct situation for yourself while ensuring Alessia remains comfortable throughout her service?

4 communicating for success

Building and honing your communications and human relations skills are important for many reasons—to build a clientele, to get along with your coworkers and managers, and to be able to articulate yourself and your ideas fully. In the following exercises you will begin to understand how to communicate with your clients and co-workers to create a fun and successful work environment!

Key Terms

communication double puzzle

Unscramble the key terms below and write the term inside the cells, by using the definitions shown.

TICLEN SOUNAL TOCNIT

⬜⬜⬜⬜⬜⬜ ⬜⬜⬜⬜⬜⬜⬜⬜⬜⬜⬜
＿＿＿16＿＿ ＿2＿＿＿＿＿＿＿＿11＿12

MLEEOEPY NIOLAVTUEA

⬜⬜⬜⬜⬜⬜⬜⬜ ⬜⬜⬜⬜⬜⬜⬜⬜⬜⬜
＿＿3＿ ＿＿＿＿＿＿7＿＿＿

CEILNT NASLOCITTUON FROM

⬜⬜⬜⬜⬜⬜ ⬜⬜⬜⬜⬜⬜⬜⬜⬜⬜⬜ ⬜⬜⬜⬜
＿＿14＿ ＿＿＿15＿＿10＿＿ ＿＿＿4

NIMMIUNOCCAOT

⬜⬜⬜⬜⬜⬜⬜⬜⬜⬜⬜⬜⬜
＿＿＿5＿＿＿＿13＿＿

RYCAFLI

⬜⬜⬜⬜⬜⬜⬜
1＿9＿＿17

TECVILEFRE TIIGLNESN

⬜⬜⬜⬜⬜⬜⬜⬜⬜ ⬜⬜⬜⬜⬜⬜⬜⬜⬜
＿＿＿8＿＿＿

Clues

1 Verbal communication with a client to determine the desired result of a service.

2 Periodic assessment of an employee's skills, attitudes and behaviors and how they are used and perceived in the salon setting.

3 A questionnaire used to gather information about a clients needs, history and preferences; filled in before the client's first service is performed at the salon.

4 The act of accurately sharing information between two people or groups of people so that it is effectively understood.

5 To make clear.

6 Listening to the client and then repeating, in your own words, what you think the client is telling you.

⬜⬜⬜⬜⬜⬜⬜⬜⬜⬜⬜⬜⬜ ⬜⬜ ⬜K⬜ !
1 2 3 4 5 6 7 8 9 10 11 12 13　14 15　16 17

Human Relations

the golden rules of human relations

Fill in the blanks below to the golden rules of human relations. Then find your answers in the word find puzzle.

1. Communicate from your _____; troubleshoot from your

   _____.

2. A _____ is far more valuable than a _____ or

   _____.

3. It is easy to make an _____; it is harder to keep a _____.

4. Ask for _____ instead of just _____.

5. Show people you care by _____ to them.

6. Tell people how _____ they are, even if they're not

   _____ that way.

7. Being _____ is different from acting _____.

8. For every _____ you do for others, do something for _____.

9. _____ often.

10. Show _____ with other people's flaws.

11. Build shared _____.

12. _____ is the best relationship builder.

```
E M D Z S R Y F L V G E E J S
Q B I M E M L A I N P C C U J
Q R I E E E U A I T Q N I E Y
T L N N S G D T M N D E V R W
E S E R H N C N R Y A I R I R
W G U Q M A W C E F E T E G G
L O Z C E Z O O E I H A S H I
Y I S R P L E H R C R P N T F
L I S T E N I N G F X F H G D
D G G O A L S E S F R H O N P
I R H V A M P T Y T A C F I I
K E T E S U O E T H G I R T Z
E A R B V K Y M T Y J K Z C Y
V T Y P L L A V L M U D C A Y
J V C C B U J H R K T R A E H
```

Communication Basics

in your own words

Explain the importance of effective communication and how you can help your client feel comfortable and welcome on their first visit.

_____

_____

_____

_____

_____

_____

_____

The Client Consultation

practice time!

Make 3 copies of the client consultation form on pages 29 and 30 and pair up with other students to complete this exercise. Have your partners pretend to be new clients, and fill out the consultation cards as if:

Client #1: Will be a bridesmaid in a wedding this Saturday.

Client #2: Is a registered nurse at the local hospital and would like a manicure and pedicure.

Client #3: Is a cosmetologist who wants the latest trend in artificial enhancements.

Once your partner fills out the consultation forms, perform each consultation separately. Follow the steps below to practice a client consultation.

Tech **Tip:**

Remember to have a pencil ready to make notes on the back of the client consultation form.

1. Escort your client to your nail station. Ensure their comfort and begin to review the consultation form.

2. Assess your client's nails and make notes.

3. Ask the history of your client's nails and past services she's had and her likes and dislikes of these services.

4. Determine the ideal length and shape and discuss this with your client.

5. Ask about your client's lifestyle to determine the correct service, length and shape.

6. Ask the client to show you a photo or explain the results she expects to achieve upon completion of the service.

7. Make suggestions on what you feel would be best after evaluating everything you have learned about her thus far.

Tech **Tip:**

Use reflective listening so the client knows you understand her wants and needs.

8. Suggest an additional service if you feel it's needed or appropriate, such as a wrap repair for a split or an extension of a broken nail.

9. Discuss what the upkeep will be of the services you have discussed.

10. Repeat what you have agreed on to ensure that your client understands exactly what the end result will be as well as the cost.

11. Repeat steps 1-10 for the other 2 clients.

CLIENT CONSULTATION FORM

Dear Client,

Our sincerest hope is to serve you with the best nail care services you've ever received! We want you to be happy with today's visit, and we also want to build a long-lasting relationship filled with trust and complete satisfaction with our services. In order for us to do this, we would like to learn more about you, your nail care needs, and your preferences. Please take a moment to answer the questions below as completely and as accurately as possible.

Thank you and we look forward to building a "beautiful" relationship!

Name

Address _____

_____

Phone Numbers: Day _____ Evening _____

Mobile _____

Email Address: _____

What is your preferred method of communication?

_____

Gender: _____Male _____Female

How did you hear about our salon? _____

If you were referred to our salon, who referred you?

_____

Please answer the following questions in the spaces provided. Thanks!

1. Approximately when was your last nail care service?

_____

2. In the past year, have you had any of the following services done either in or out of a salon?

_____Manicure _____Pedicure

_____ Nail Enhancements _____Other

3. It is important that you discuss with your nail technician any chronic condition(s) you may have, so that precautions can be considered. Examples of conditions would be circulatory diseases, diabetes, peripheral artery disease (PAD), arthritis, high blood pressure, and others.

4. How would you characterize your natural nails?

_____Normal _____Strong

_____Brittle _____Flexible

_____Other

5. Do you regularly receive any of the following nail services?
(Check all that apply):

_____Monomer and Polymer Nail Enhancements

_____Monomer and Polymer Nail Enhancements with UV Gel Overlay

_____UV Gel Nail Enhancements

_____Fabric Wraps (Circle Type: Silk, Linen, or Fiberglass)

_____Manicure

_____Natural Nail Treatments

_____Paraffin Hand Treatments

6. Do you receive any of the following foot services? (Check all that apply):

_____Basic Pedicure   _____Spa Pedicure

_____Masks or Paraffin Foot Treatments

7. Please share information about your most successful and least successful types
of nail services. _____
_____

8. What types of frequent activities do you engage in that could cause damage to
your nails? _____
_____

9. What are you goals for today's nail appointment? _____
_____

10. Do you have a special occasion coming up in the near future where your nails
must look their absolute best? If so, when?

Quick Review!

chapter 4: communicating for success

Complete the multiple-choice questions below by circling the correct answer to each question.

1. What are some good ways to handle the ups and downs of human relations?
   a. Respond instead of reacting.
   b. Believe in yourself.
   c. Talk less, listen more.
   d. All of the above

2. The best way to understand others is to begin with a firm understanding of
   a. Their past history
   b. Their personality
   c. Yourself
   d. A and B

3. Good relationships are built on what?
   a. Mutual respect
   b. Understanding
   c. Love
   d. A and B

4. What is the single most important part of any service?
   a. Cleaning
   b. Polish
   c. Client consultation
   d. Massage

5. A fundamental factor in human relations has to do with what?
   a. How much money we have
   b. How secure we are feeling
   c. How we feel that day
   d. How much we care for the other

6. You can help people feel secure around you by being
   a. Respectful
   b. Trustworthy
   c. Honest
   d. All of the above

7. How often should a client consultation be performed, to some degree?
   a. Only on the first visit to the salon.
   b. At every single service and salon visit.
   c. When getting a new service performed.
   d. A and C

8. If you have a client that is habitually late, which of the following can help you to lessen the disruption to your schedule and your clientele?
    a. Schedule your tardy client as the last client of the day
    b. Tell your tardy client that her appointment is earlier than you have scheduled it for.
    c. Book in additional time for your tardy client so if she's late you still have enough time to complete her service.
    d. A or B

9. What is the number-one thing to remember when a scheduling mix-up occurs?
    a. Accommodate the guest in every way, even if it means having her serviced by another nail technician in your salon.
    b. Stay calm and reschedule.
    c. Be polite and never argue about who is correct.
    d. Find who's to blame and then fix the problem.

10. When dealing with an unhappy client, what is the first thing you should do?
    a. Refer to your manager on how to proceed.
    b. Find out exactly what she is unhappy about and try to fix it.
    c. Refer the unhappy client to a more experienced nail technician in your salon.
    d. Reschedule your client for another time when you can fix the mistakes and give her a free service.

11. When communicating with your colleagues you will want to
    a. Remain objective
    b. Treat everyone with respect
    c. Remain neutral
    d. All of the above.

12. The salon community is usually a close-knit one in which people spend long hours working side by side. For this reason, it is important to
    a. Keep to yourself
    b. Become friends with everyone
    c. Maintain boundaries
    d. All of the above

13. Before communicating with your salon manager, you may want to,
    a. Have your complaints and issues written down.
    b. Make sure you have all the facts correct.
    c. Discuss the meeting with your coworkers
    d. None of the above.

14. What is the job of the salon manager?
    a. To make decisions that are best for the salon as a whole.
    b. To solve personal issues between staff members.
    c. To listen to staff members vent.
    d. All of the above.

15. What types of questions are NOT appropriate to ask at an evaluation meeting?

    a. When can I take on more services?
    b. When will my pay be increased?
    c. When might I be considered for promotion?
    d. When can I take my next vacation?

what would you do?   a salon **scenario**

Your long-time client Audrey is 20 minutes late for her appointment as usual. Although her spa pedicure will only take one hour, Margo, your next appointment, is scheduled in 45 minutes. What would you do in this scenario?

_____

_____

_____

_____

_____

_____

_____

_____

_____

_____

_____

Part2

GENERAL SCIENCES

5 infection
control:
PRINCIPLES AND PRACTICES

Keep it CLEAN—you'll understand why after you finish with this chapter! Now we'll review how to protect yourself and your clients from those nasty germs and why "keeping it clean" is for more than just looks!

Key Terms

infection control key words puzzle

Fill in the crossword puzzle with key words found in chapter 5 by using the clues below.

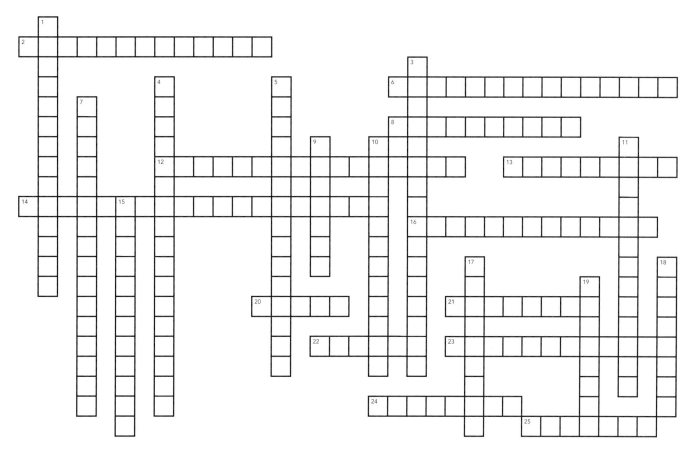

ACROSS

2 Not harmful; organisms that may perform useful functions.

6 Immunity that is partly inherited and partly developed through healthy living.

8 Causing disease; may cause harmful conditions or illnesses in humans.

12 Immunity that the body develops after overcoming a disease through inoculation (such as flu vaccinations) or through exposure to natural allergens, such as pollen, cat dander, and ragweed.

13 The invasion of body tissues by pathogens.

14 Illness resulting from conditions associated with employment, such as prolonged and repeated overexposure to certain products or ingredients.

16 The presence, or the reasonably anticipated presence, of blood or other potentially infectious materials on an item's surface, or visible debris/residues such as dust, hair, skin, etc.

20 Nonscientific synonyms for disease-producing bacteria.

21 One-celled microorganisms with both plant and animal characteristics.

22 Any of various poisonous substances, produced by some microorganisms (bacteria and viruses).

23 Condition in which a part of the body reacts to protect itself from injury, irritation, or infection, and is characterized by redness, heat, pain, and swelling.

24 Self-movement.

25 Reaction due to extreme sensitivity to certain foods, chemicals, or other normally harmless substances.

1 An infection, such as a pimple or abscess, that is confined to a particular part of the body and is indicated by a lesion containing pus.

3 Disease caused by parasites, such as lice and ringworm.

4 Disease that is transmittable by contact.

5 Disease that affects the body generally, often due to under- or over-functioning of internal glands/organs.

7 Contact with non-intact skin, blood, body fluid or other potentially infection materials that results from performance of an employee's duties

9 Abnormal condition of all or part of the body, organ, or mind that makes it incapable of carrying on normal function.

10 A disease caused by bacteria that is only transmitted through coughing.

11 Any organism of microscopic or submicroscopic size.

15 Showing no symptoms or signs of infection.

17 Determination of the nature of a disease from its symptoms. Federal regulations prohibit salon professionals from performing this.

18 The ability of the body to destroy and resist infection; can be either natural or acquired and is a sign of good health.

19 An organism that grows, feeds, and shelters on or in another organism, while contributing nothing to the survival of that organism (referred to as the host).

Principles of Infection

recognizing bacteria

Use the memory cards to help identify the bacteria descriptions below. Fill in the correct bacteria name next to the description.

1. _____ Pus-forming bacteria arranged in curved lines resembling a string of beads.

2. _____ Short rod-shaped bacteria.

3. _____ Round-shaped bacteria that appear singly (alone) or in groups.

4. _____ Spiral or corkscrew-shaped bacteria.

5. _____ Pus-forming bacteria that grow in clusters like a bunch of grapes.

6. _____ Slender, hairlike extensions used by bacilli and spirilla for locomotion also known as cilia.

7. _____ Microscopic plant parasites, including molds, mildews, and yeasts.

8. _____ Spherical bacteria that grow in pairs and cause diseases such as pneumonia.

identifying bacteria

This matching memory game can be played alone, but it's more fun with other students! Cut out the bacteria memory cards and turn them over so the pictures face down. Mix them up and take turns turning the cards over trying to match them with their pair. The person with the most matches at the end of the game wins!

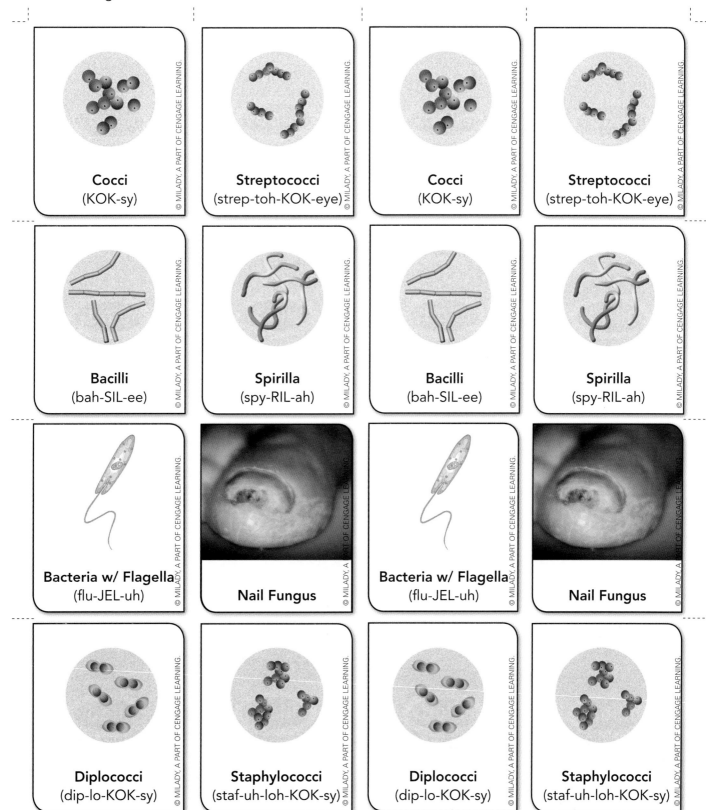

Cocci
(KOK-sy)

Streptococci
(strep-toh-KOK-eye)

Cocci
(KOK-sy)

Streptococci
(strep-toh-KOK-eye)

Bacilli
(bah-SIL-ee)

Spirilla
(spy-RIL-ah)

Bacilli
(bah-SIL-ee)

Spirilla
(spy-RIL-ah)

Bacteria w/ Flagella
(flu-JEL-uh)

Nail Fungus

Bacteria w/ Flagella
(flu-JEL-uh)

Nail Fungus

Diplococci
(dip-lo-KOK-sy)

Staphylococci
(staf-uh-loh-KOK-sy)

Diplococci
(dip-lo-KOK-sy)

Staphylococci
(staf-uh-loh-KOK-sy)

© MILADY, A PART OF CENGAGE LEARNING.

identifying bacteria (continued)

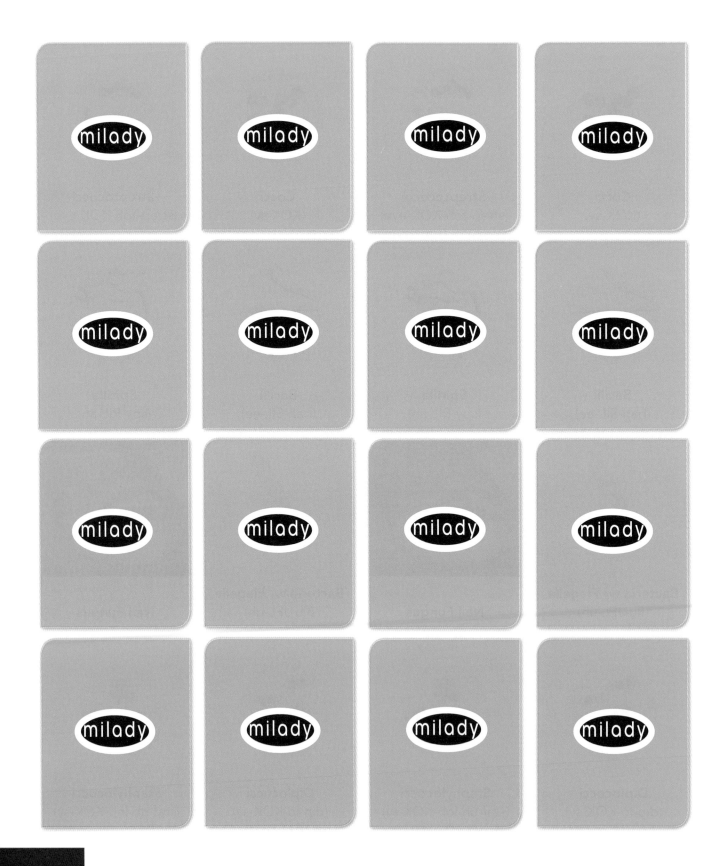

infection facts

Circle true or false about the statements below about infections in the salon.

T   F   **1.** A virus is capable of replication only through taking over the host cell's reproduction machinery.

T   F   **2.** Fungi affects plants or grows on inanimate objects, but does not cause human infections in the salon.

T   F   **3.** Hepatitis B is a bloodborne virus that causes disease affecting the liver.

T   F   **4.** HIV can live on a surface outside the body for long periods of time.

T   F   **5.** Ringworm is another contagious skin disease that is caused by the itch mite, which burrows under the skin

need to know!

Below, identify what each acronym stands for and describe the important role plays it plays in the nail salon.

1. EPA _____

_____

2. MSDS _____

_____

_____

_____

_____

3. AIDS _____

_____

4. OSHA _____

_____

_____

5. MRSA _____

_____

_____

6. HIV _____

_____

7. HPV _____

_____

_____

8. CDC _____

_____

State Board Exam NOTES!

Some states require that all procedures for cleaning and disinfecting pedicure equipment be recorded in a salon pedicure logbook. Check with your regulatory agency to determine whether you are required to do so. It is a good practice even if not required and shows clients you're serious about protecting their health.

spreading bacteria and viruses

Name nine ways that bacteria and viruses can be spread in a salon situation.

1. _____

2. _____

3. _____

4. _____

5. _____

6. _____

7. _____

8. _____

9. _____

decontamination

Stop the spread of these viruses and bacteria with three steps of decontamination! Define what these important procedures do.

1. Sterilization: _____

_____

2. Disinfection: _____

_____

_____

3. Cleaning: _____

_____

Laws and Regulations

salon cleanliness

Circle true or false about the statements below about laws and regulations and infections in the salon.

T   F   **1.** Laws or statutes are written by both the federal and state legislatures that determine the scope of practice (what each license allows the holder to do) and establish guidelines for regulatory agencies to make rules.

T   F   **2.** Rules or regulations are written by the regulatory agency or state board and determine how the law will be applied and establish specific standards of conduct.

T   F   **3.** Disinfectants are **not** for use on human skin, hair, or nails.

T   F   **4.** Disinfectants used in salons must be bactericidal, capable of destroying bacteria, fungicidal, capable of destroying fungi, and virucidal, capable of destroying viruses.

T   F   **5.** Cleaning is the process that completely destroys all microbial life, including spores, and is necessary only when surgical instruments cut into the vascular layers of the body (this does not mean an accidental cut).

State Board Exam NOTES!

Federal agencies set guidelines for manufacturing, sale, and use of equipment and chemical ingredients, and for safety in the workplace, place limits on the types of services you can perform in the salon. **State agencies** regulate licensing, enforcement, and your conduct when working in the salon.

chapter 5: infection control: principles and practice review

Complete the multiple-choice questions below by circling the correct answer to each question.

1. What are four types of potentially infectious microorganisms that are important to nail technicians?
   a. Bacteria, HIV, fungi, and hepatitis
   b. Bacteria, fungi, viruses and parasites.
   c. Spirilla, cocci, bacilli, flagella
   d. Fungi, HPV, HIV, hepatitis

2. What is an example of a bloodborne pathogen?
   a. HPV
   b. Hepatitis
   c. HIV
   d. B and C

3. Both bacterial and fungal infections can be spread to other nails, or to other clients, unless everything that touches the client is:
   a. Properly disposed of (disposable or single use items)
   b. Properly cleaned and disinfected before reuse
   c. Properly placed in a dry, cleaned area before and after use
   d. A and B

4. Pathogenic bacteria, viruses or fungi can enter the body through:
   a. Broken skin
   b. The mouth
   c. The nose
   d. All of the above

5. The spread of disease-causing microorganisms such as hepatitis and HIV are possible when:
   a. Giving a massage
   b. When clients and technicians do not wash their hands
   c. Coughing or sneezing
   d. Any time the skin is broken

6. Disinfectants must be registered with the _____ and will have a registration number on the label.
   a. CDC
   b. EPA
   c. FDA
   d. OSHA

7. When you purchase a disinfectant for the salon to eliminate specific germs, what must it have on the label?
   a. MSDS
   b. Efficacy claims
   c. Alcohol content
   d. A hospital grade seal

8. Generally, how many minutes should a disinfectant be in/on a surface, implement or footbath to properly disinfect it?
   a. 5 minutes
   b. For as long as recommended by the product's manufacturer
   c. 15 minutes
   d. For as long as recommended by the FDA

9. What dangerous chemical used to sterilize surgical instruments in hospitals is not safe for salon use?
   a. Sodium hypochlorite
   b. Phenolics
   c. Quaternary ammonium compounds
   d. Glutaraldehyde

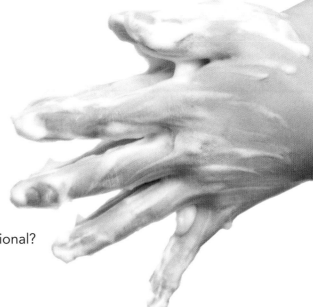

10. What is one of the most important actions you can use to prevent spreading germs from one person to another?
    a. Taking a shower
    b. Washing your hands
    c. Sterilizing
    d. Covering your mouth when you cough or sneeze

11. What is your most important responsibility as a salon professional?
    a. Maintaining happy clients
    b. Creating perfect nail enhancements
    c. Protecting your clients' health and safety
    d. Getting along with co-workers and clients

12. _____ are published by OSHA, and require that employers and employees assume that all human blood and body fluids are infectious.
    a. Universal Precautions
    b. MSDS
    c. Exposure Incidents
    d. Statutes

13. Chemical germicides formulated for use on skin and registered and regulated by the FDA are called:
    a. Bactericidal
    b. Antiseptics
    c. Disinfectants
    d. Quats

14. The process that completely destroys all microbial life, including spores is:
   a. Disinfection
   b. Cleaning
   c. Sterilization
   d. Sanitizing

15. A substance designed to prevent hard water from reducing the effectiveness of cleaners and disinfectants is called:
   a. Chelating agent
   b. Bleach
   c. Hard water tablets
   d. Antiseptic solution

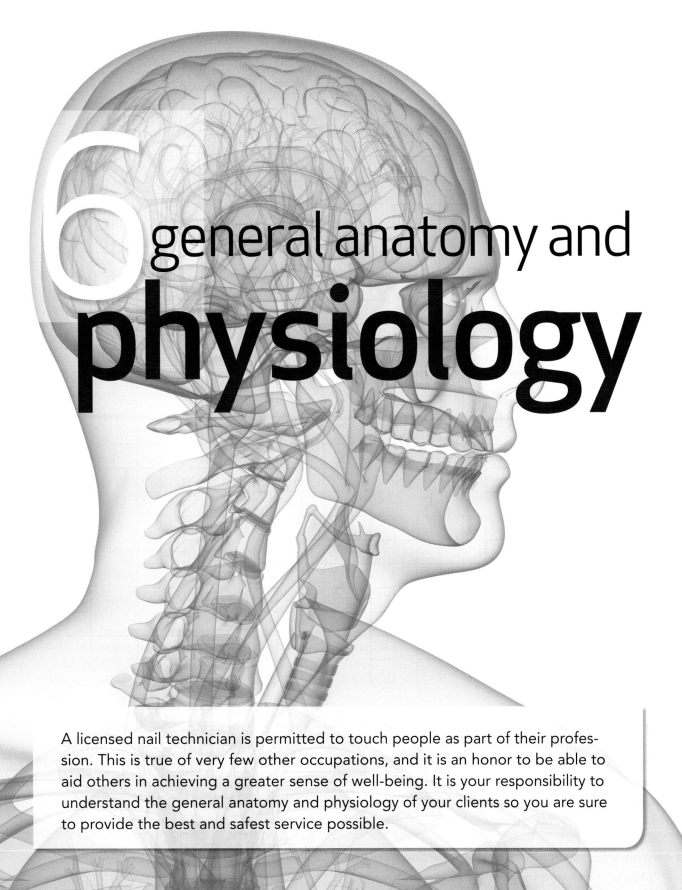

6 general anatomy and physiology

A licensed nail technician is permitted to touch people as part of their profession. This is true of very few other occupations, and it is an honor to be able to aid others in achieving a greater sense of well-being. It is your responsibility to understand the general anatomy and physiology of your clients so you are sure to provide the best and safest service possible.

Key Terms

the body crossword

Fill in the crossword puzzle with key words found in chapter 6, by using the clues below.

ACROSS

1 Structure that temporarily closes a passage or permits blood flow in one direction only.

5 Special structures found inside the lymphatic vessels that filter lymph.

9 Whitish cord made up of bundles of nerve fibers held together by connective tissue, through which impulses are transmitted.

13 Muscle of the chest that assists in breathing and in raising the arm.

16 The involuntary muscle that is the heart. This type of muscle is not found in any other part of the body.

17 Groups of bodily organs acting together to perform one or more functions. The human body is composed of 11 of these.

19 Chemical process that takes place in living organisms through which the cells are nourished and carry out their activities.

22 Act of breathing; the exchange of carbon dioxide and oxygen in the lungs and within each cell.
24 Bone.
25 Connection between two or more bones of the skeleton.
26 Specialized organ that removes certain constituents from the blood to convert them into new substances.
31 One of the two lower chambers of the heart.
32 Thin-walled blood vessel that is less elastic than an artery.
33 A finger or toe.

DOWN

2 Clear fluid that carries waste and impurities away from the cells.
3 Body organs that control the body's vision.
4 Muscular cone-shaped organ that keeps the blood moving within the circulatory system.
5 Another term for white blood cells.
6 Thick-walled, muscular, flexible tubes that carry oxygenated blood away from the heart to the capillaries.
7 One of the two upper chambers of the heart through which blood is pumped to the ventricles.
8 Muscular wall that separates the thorax from the abdominal region and helps control breathing.
10 The largest artery in the body.
11 Blood plasma found in the spaces between tissues.
12 Tiny, thin-walled blood vessel that connects the smaller arteries to the veins.
14 Portion of the central nervous system that originates in the brain, extends down to the lower extremity of the trunk, and is protected by the spinal column.
15 Part of the central nervous system contained in the cranium; largest and most complex nerve tissue; controls sensation, muscles, gland activity, and the power to think and feel emotions.
18 Nerves that carry impulses from the brain to the muscles.
20 Coloring matter of the blood; a complex iron protein in red blood cells that binds to oxygen.
21 Secretion, such as insulin, adrenalin, and estrogen, produced by one of the endocrine glands and carried by the bloodstream or body fluid to another part of the body to stimulate a specific activity.
23 A body organ that, along with the stomach, digests food.
27 Organs of respiration; spongy tissues composed of microscopic cells in which inhaled air is exchanged for carbon dioxide during one breathing cycle.
28 Automatic reaction to a stimulus that involves the movement of an impulse from a sensory receptor along the sensory nerve to the spinal cord.
29 Major body organ that, along with the intestines, digests food.
30 Body organs that excrete water and waste products.

histology double puzzle

Identify theses terms about cell structure and reproduction using the definitions and write your answer in the space provided. Copy the letters in the numbered cells to the other cells with the same number to reveal the secret message!

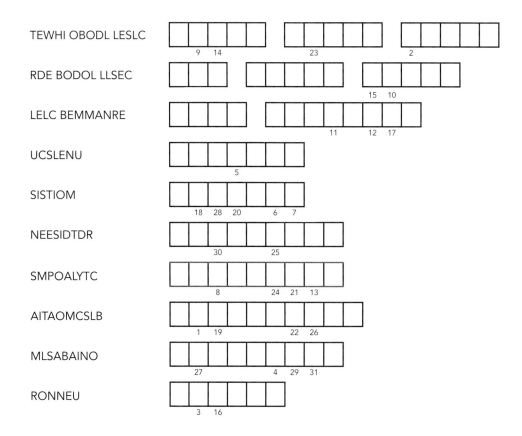

TEWHI OBODL LESLC — 9 14 | 23 | 2

RDE BODOL LLSEC — 15 10

LELC BEMMANRE — 11 12 17

UCSLENU — 5

SISTIOM — 18 28 20 6 7

NEESIDTDR — 30 25

SMPOALYTC — 8 24 21 13

AITAOMCSLB — 1 19 22 26

MLSABAINO — 27 4 29 31

RONNEU — 3 16

Clues

1 Also called white corpuscles or leukocytes; blood cells that perform the function of destroying disease-causing microorganisms.

2 Blood cells that carry oxygen from the lungs to the body cells and transport carbon dioxide from the cells back to the lungs.

3 Cell part that encloses the protoplasm and permits soluble substances to enter and leave the cell.

4 Dense, active protoplasm found in the center of the cell; plays an important part in cell reproduction and metabolism.

5 Cells dividing into two new cells (daughter cells); the usual process of cell reproduction of human tissues.

6 Tree-like branching of nerve fibers extending from a nerve cell; short nerve fibers that carry impulses toward the cell and receive impulses from other neurons

7. The protoplasm of a cell, except that which is in the nucleus; the watery fluid that cells need for growth, reproduction, and self-repair.

8. The phase of metabolism that involves the breaking down of complex compounds within the cells into smaller ones. This process releases energy that has been stored.

9. Constructive metabolism; the process of building up larger molecules from smaller ones.

10. Nerve cell; primary structural unit of the nervous system, consisting of cell body, nucleus, dendrites, and axon.

Fun Fact...

An individual blood cell takes about 60 seconds to make a complete circuit of the body.

Source: http://www.corsinet.com/trivia/h-triv.html

draw this!

In the box below draw a nerve cell. Be sure and include the nucleus, cell body, dendrites and axon.

types of tissue

Tissue is a collection of similar cells that perform a specific function and can be recognized by its characteristic appearance. Describe the four types of tissue in the body in the space provided.

1. Connective tissue

_____

_____

_____

_____

_____

2. Epithelial tissue

_____

_____

_____

_____

_____

3. Muscular tissue

_____

_____

_____

_____

_____

4. Nerve tissue

_____

_____

_____

_____

_____

Basic Physiology

body systems

Match the major systems of the human body to their descriptions.

_____ **1.** Reproductive

_____ **2.** Integumentary

_____ **3.** Endocrine

_____ **4.** Digestive

_____ **5.** Circulatory

_____ **6.** Muscular

_____ **7.** Lymphatic/immune

_____ **8.** Excretory

_____ **9.** Respiratory

_____ **10.** Nervous

_____ **11.** Skeletal

a. Purifies the body by eliminating waste matter

b. Protective covering that also helps regulate body temperature

c. Pertaining to the heart, blood vessels, and the circulation of blood

d. Changes food into nutrients and wastes

e. Ductless glands that regulate bodily functions via hormones secreted into the bloodstream

f. System that allows the body to move internally and externally

g. Controls and coordinates all other systems

h. Specific organs that regulate all sexual functioning

i. Enables breathing, supplies the body with oxygen, and eliminates carbon dioxide as a waste product

j. The physical foundation of the body

k. It carries waste and impurities away from the cells.

Fun **Fact...**

Babies are born with 300 bones, but by adulthood we have only 206 in our bodies.

Source: http://www.corsinet.com/trivia/h-triv.html

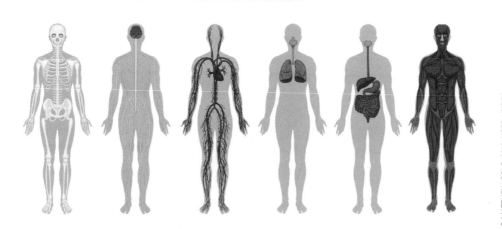

Basic Anatomy

where are these bones?

Using the names of the bones of the hand, arm, shoulder, foot, ankle, and leg listed below, write in the correct name that points to the bone on the following drawings.

Tech Tip:

Phalanges are located in the hand and foot.

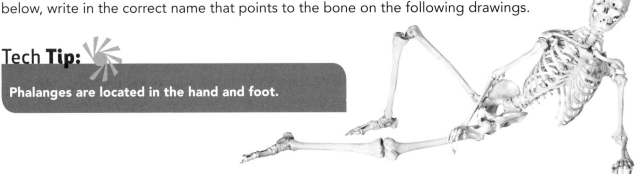

Calcaneus	Femur	Middle phalanx	Radius
Carpus	Fibula	Navicular	Talus
Cuboid	Humerus	Patella	Tibia
Cuneiforms	Interfalangeal joints	Phalanges	Ulna
Distal phalanx	Metacarpus	Proximal phalanx	
Distal phalanx of Great Toe	Metatarsals	Proximal phalanx of Great Toe	

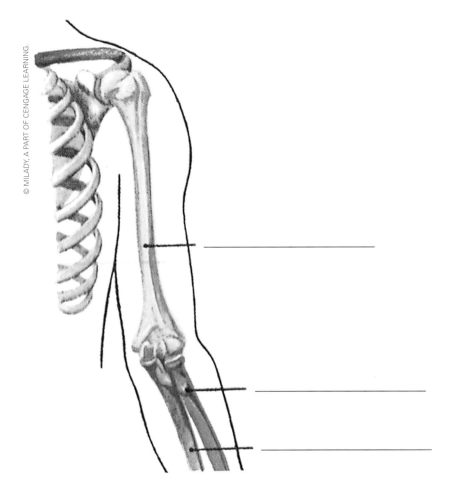

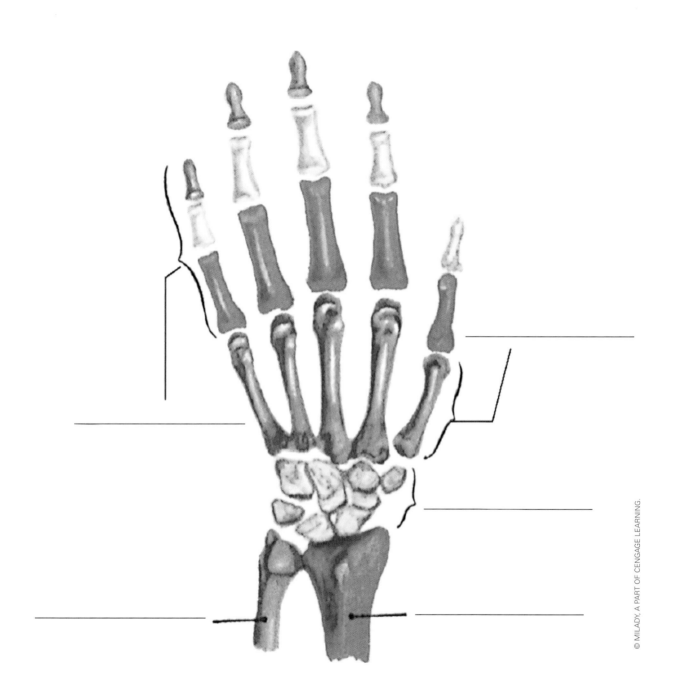

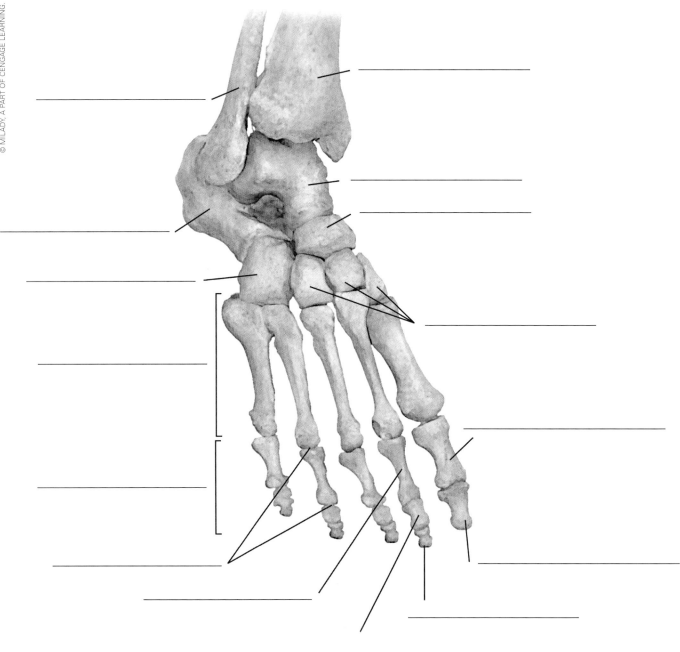

Fun **Fact...**

There are 206 bones in the body. 26 of them are in the feet.

Source: http://www.ehow.com

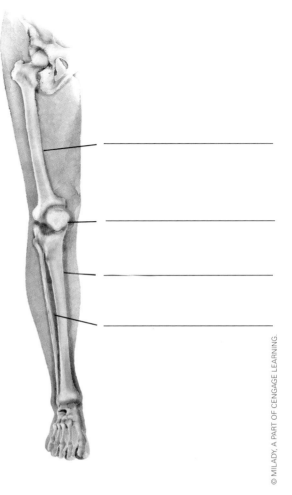

State Board Exam **NOTES**

There is a good chance that you will need to identify these bones during your state licensing written exam. It may be helpful to retest yourself on this material multiple times before your test.

muscles

Name the muscles of the shoulder, arm, hand, leg and foot, by using the clues given. Then find the muscles in the word find puzzle on page 59.

_____   **1.** Muscle that turns the hand inward so that the palm faces downward.

_____   **2.** Muscle that covers the outer side of the calf and inverts the foot and turns it outward.

_____   **3.** Large triangular muscle covering the shoulder joint that allows the arm to extend outward and to the side of the body.

_____   **4.** Muscle producing the contour of the front and inner side of the upper arm; it lifts the forearm and flexes the elbow.

_____   **5.** Muscles that separate the fingers and the toes.

_____   **6.** Muscle that originates on the lower surface of the fibula. It bends the foot down and out.

_____ **7.** Muscle of the foot that moves the toes and help maintain balance while walking and standing.

_____ **8.** Muscle that bends the foot up and extends the toes.

_____ **9.** Muscle at the base of each finger that draws the fingers together.

_____ **10.** Muscle that is attached to the lower rear surface of the heel and pulls the foot down.

_____ **11.** Extensor muscle of the wrist involved in flexing the wrist.

_____ **12.** Muscle of the foot that moves the toes and help maintain balance.

_____ **13.** Muscle that straightens the wrist, hand, and fingers to form a straight line.

_____ **14.** Muscle that covers the back of the neck and upper and middle region of the back; rotates and controls swinging movements of the arm.

_____ **15.** Large muscle that covers the entire back of the upper arm and extends the forearm.

_____ **16.** Muscle that covers the front of the shin. It bends the foot upward and inward.

_____ **17.** Muscle of the forearm that rotates the radius outward and the palm upward.

_____ **18.** Muscle that originates at the upper portion of the fibula and bends the foot down.

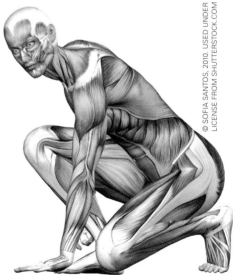

Fun Fact...

The human body has over 600 muscles, 40% of the body's weight.

```
H B K X S R G Q L T Z T T D E O K T O I V O N J D
P U Q E I A O C C Y J R I B X K K R G G B C L E C
L E V R V Q F X F H O I B C T S T A P D H Z J T B
K D M C E N B A E R N C I D E V K P J Z J U D A P
I J C I R D H Z A L N E A F N F P E A J Z U F S G
F P Y W B V I P R Q F P L W S V G Z M B K I A C O
G I H S M R A O Z P S F I F O G T I H O P T H D Q
N O S I U X Z V T O H G S B R R B U L X I K A S J
U J L C R G H P L L T Q A I D A O S L N F P O I K
I Q L U O D F E F Q E C N C I Y B T M N Q H Y Z W
Q X K L T B U C P K D D T E G S U D A F Q L H O B
Z N Q L I S B Q O N O V E P I U D T U N J F Y Q U
W P C A G O P M J A N E R N T I L V S C I R S Y R
V F W H I A T X R I F V I I O M J K Q W T P W S P
R N O R D Q B H T S A R O W R E U P M K S O U Q M
Q W X O R S B I Q O O N R D U N W Z X E J Y R S F
B O X T O T I G T T U V A T M C P R O N A T O R E
Q D C C X J T V C E W L P Q L O E X T E N S O R M
S T L U E H X U O C O U C G O R B Q V P N S F X N
A M K D L I D H A E G A M E N T G B P J N I A S P
Q M E B F D S B F G D H L D G S A H M B M K S W U
L B W A A X C P W D U M O K U A N B Y G B F J O N
S U G N O L S U E N O R E P S G B N E V X R Y A F
K A D E X T E N S O R D I G I T O R U M D I K S C
E R T U S I V E R B S U E N O R E P E Y I B P G A
```

chapter 6: general anatomy and physiology

Complete the multiple-choice questions below by circling the correct answer to each question.

1. Tissue that gives smoothness and contour to the body is called:
   a. Adipose tissue
   b. Nerve tissue
   c. Connective tissue
   d. Epithelial tissue

2. What is the name of the nutritive fluid that flows through the circulatory system and that supplies oxygen and nutrients to cells and tissues?
   a. Plasma
   b. Liquid tissue
   c. Hemoglobin
   d. Blood

3. What is an example of connective tissue?
   a. Bone, cartilage, and ligaments
   b. Tendons and fat
   c. Muscle, tissue, and lymph
   d. A and B

4. _____ helps maintain balance while walking and standing.
   a. Brevis
   b. Muscles
   c. Tendons
   d. B and C

5. The layer of tissue covering the whole muscle trunk is called the:
   a. Skin
   b. Fascia
   c. Plasma
   d. None of the above

6. The study of tiny structures found in tissues is called:
   a. Neurology
   b. Osteology
   c. Histology
   d. Anatomy

7. The study of the nature, structure, function, and diseases of the muscles is called:
   a. Myology
   b. Physiology
   c. Neurology
   d. Osteology

8. The study of anatomy, structure, and function of the bones is called:
   a. Physiology
   b. Neurology
   c. Osteology
   d. Anatomy

9. _____ is the fluid part of the blood that carries food and other useful substances to the cells.
   a. Platelets
   b. Water
   c. Plasma
   d. None of the above

10. Which is the blood cell that aids in the forming of clots?
   a. Platelet
   b. Plasma
   c. White blood cell
   d. Red blood cell

11. What major organ is the external protective coating of the body?
   a. Skin
   b. Muscle
   c. Fascia
   d. None of the above.

12. Muscles that are voluntarily or consciously controlled are called:
   a. Nonstriated muscle
   b. Striated muscle
   c. Cardiac muscle
   d. None of the above

13. A "system" is comprised of a group of _____ acting together to perform one or more functions.
   a. Tissues
   b. Muscles
   c. Body organs
   d. All of the above

14. _____ is the study of the human body structures that can be seen with the naked eye, and what they are made up of. It is the science of the structure of organisms or of their parts.
   a. Anatomy
   b. Physiology
   c. Neurology
   d. Osteology

15. Tissue is a collection of _____ that perform a particular function.
   a. Fascia
   b. Fat
   c. Similar cells
   d. Muscles

skin structure and growth

When treating the hands, arms, feet, and calves, nail technicians will inevitably encounter skin disorders and diseases. For the safety of clients, as well as the nail technician, it is important to be able to recognize contagious conditions, and those requiring medical care.

skin key words puzzle

Fill in the crossword puzzle with key words found in Chapter 7, by using the clues below.

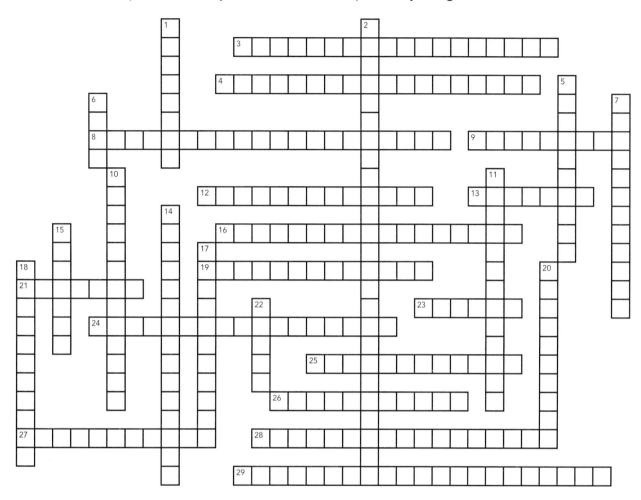

ACROSS

3 Most common and least severe type of skin cancer; often characterized by light or pearly nodules.

4 Sensory receptors that send messages to the brain. These react to heat, cold, touch, pressure, and pain.

8 Fibers that are distributed to the sweat and oil glands.

9 Chemicals released in the blood that enlarge the vessels around an injury so that blood can speed removal of any allergy-causing substance.

12 Excessive sweating caused by heat or general body weakness.

13 Fiber protein that is the principal component of hair and nails.

16 Most serious form of skin cancer; often characterized by black or dark brown patches on the skin that may appear uneven in texture, jagged, or raised.

19 A tube-like duct that is part of the sudoriferous gland. It ends at the surface of the skin to form the sweat pore.

21 Protein base similar to collagen that forms elastic tissue.

23 Spot or discoloration on the skin, such as a freckle. The spot is neither raised nor sunken.

24 Small epidermal structures with nerve endings that are sensitive to touch and pressure.

25 Foul-smelling perspiration, usually noticeable in the armpits or on the feet.

26 Medical branch of science that deals with the study of skin and its nature, structure, functions, diseases, and treatment.
27 Skin sore or abrasion produced by scratching or scraping.
28 An eruptive skin infection caused by touching certain substances to the skin; maybe short-term or long-term.
29 Type of skin cancer more serious than basal cell carcinoma; often characterized by scaly red papules or nodules.

DOWN

1 Fibrous protein that gives the skin form and strength.
2 Skin that becomes allergic to an ingredient in a product; often caused by prolonged or repeated contact.
5 Abnormal inflammatory condition of the skin.
6 Closed, abnormally developed sac, containing fluid, semifluid, or morbid matter, above or below the skin.
7 Prolonged, repeated, or long-term exposure that can cause sensitivity.
10 Greatly increased or exaggerated allergic sensitivity to products.
11 Physician engaged in the science of treating the skin—its structures, functions, and diseases.
14 Dilation of surface blood vessels.
15 Tiny grains of pigment (coloring matter) deposited into cells in the layer of the epidermis and papillary layers of the dermis.
17 Specialist in cleansing, preservation of health, and beautification of the skin and body; one who gives therapeutic facial treatments.
18 Melanin-forming cells.
20 Deficiency in perspiration, often a result of fever or certain skin diseases.
22 Dead cells that form over a wound or blemish while it is healing; an accumulation of sebum and pus, sometimes mixed with epidermal material.

aka: also known as

These key terms have a general name and a medical or technical name. Match up the term with its AKA.

_____ **1.** Cicatrix   A. Scar

_____ **2.** Verruca   B. Subcutaneous Tissue

_____ **3.** Vesicle   C. Blister (With Clear Fluid)

_____ **4.** Adipose Tissue   D. Cuticle

_____ **5.** Sudoriferous Glands   E. Dermis

_____ **6.** Cutis   F. Sweat Glands

_____ **7.** Keratoma   G. Wart

_____ **8.** Epidermis   H. Callus

_____ **9.** Miliaria Rubra   I. Black and White Heads (pimples)

_____ **10.** Stratum Germinativum   J. Prickly Heat

_____ **11.** Comedones   K. Basal Cell Layer

Anatomy of the Skin

skin structure

Use the terms below to label the diagram of the structures of the skin.

Adipose (fatty) tissue   Epidermis   Sebaceous (oil) gland   Stratum spinosm

Arrector pili muscle   Hair Shaft   Stratum corneum   Subcutaneous tissue

Arteries   Mouth of follicle   Stratum germinativum   Sudoriferous gland

Dermal papilla   Papillary layer of dermis   Stratum granulosum   Sweat pore

Dermis (true skin)   Reticular layer of dermis   Stratum lucidum   Veins

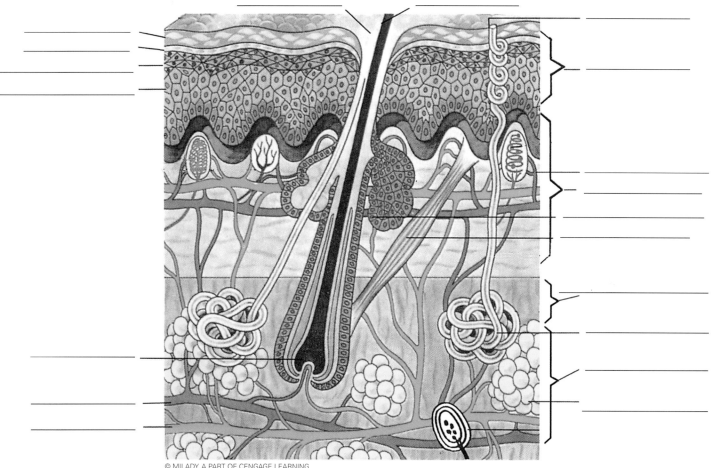

© MILADY, A PART OF CENGAGE LEARNING.

skin composition

Use the terms below to label the diagram of the structures of the skin.

Dermis   Papillary layer   Stratum corneum   Stratum germinativum

Epidermis   Reticular layer   Stratum granulosum   Stratum lucidum

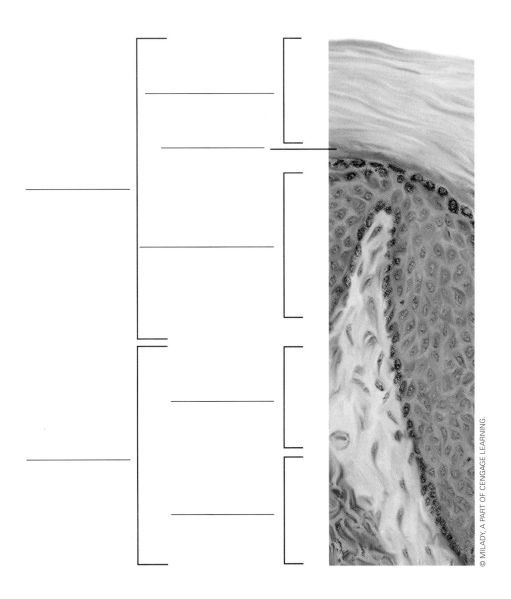

© MILADY, A PART OF CENGAGE LEARNING.

Fun Fact...

Humans shed and re-grow outer skin cells about every 27 days, totaling almost 1,000 new skins in a lifetime.

Source: http://www.corsinet.com/trivia/h-triv.html

functions of the skin

Name and explain the principal functions of the skin.

1. _____
   _____

2. _____
   _____

3. _____
   _____

4. _____
   _____

5. _____
   _____

6. _____
   _____

Maintaining Skin Health
skin health facts!

Answer true or false to the statements below.

Fun Fact...

An average human drinks about 16, 000 gallons of water in a lifetime.

T   F   **1.** Metabolism can be slowed by as much as 3%-with even mild dehydration.

T   F   **2.** Daytime fatigue is not affected by water content.

T   F   **3.** Short-term memory is related to hormones, not water.

T   F   **4.** Feelings of hunger can be lessened by drinking a glass of water.

T   F   **5.** Drinking lots of water can help stop hunger pangs for many dieters.

T   F   **6.** The best source of vitamin D is drinking milk .

T   F   **7.** Vitamin K speeds up the body's healing process.

T   F   **8.** Vitamin and mineral supplements help meet the body's daily nutritional needs.

T   F   **9.** Proper moisturizers are essential to maintaining the health of the skin.

T   F   **10.** Vitamins A, C, D, and E have been proven to positively impact the health of the skin.

Aging of the Skin

preventing premature aging puzzle

Complete the statements below by filling in the blanks, and then find and circle your answer in the word find puzzle on the next page.

1. Wear a 15 SPF, _____ sunscreen to protect your skin from sun damage.

2. Avoid prolonged sun exposure between 10:00 AM and 3:00 PM, the hours when _____ is highest.

3. Apply _____ approximately 30 minutes before going out in the sun.

4. Always reapply sunscreen after _____ or heavy _____.

5. _____ 6 months of age or younger should not be exposed to (sun).

6. Have a regular _____ check-up by a _____ to ensure that no _____ or _____ lesions are present.

7. Name four lifestyle choices that can cause skin aging.

   a. _____

   b. _____

   c. _____

   d. _____

```
L  N  K  Z  N  I  C  S  U  Q  Q  C  K  T  S  G  B  D  J  L
R  O  R  W  B  A  M  N  U  S  A  J  S  Q  U  H  R  R  P  R
G  W  H  X  M  O  C  U  Z  N  W  I  G  T  N  H  O  S  W  Q
L  Z  W  O  K  O  J  E  C  N  G  Y  G  V  S  E  A  P  Y  H
K  D  R  I  C  Z  Z  E  Y  O  Y  L  V  T  C  Q  D  G  H  E
I  N  N  P  Z  L  R  S  L  B  G  T  U  F  R  P  S  M  K  C
N  G  X  G  N  O  A  O  W  Q  S  L  C  Q  E  E  P  T  K  C
Z  S  W  B  U  Q  T  G  U  I  B  S  K  L  E  R  E  G  S  S
Q  P  G  S  K  A  X  C  N  Z  M  U  F  V  N  S  C  F  H  O
M  J  V  F  M  C  U  U  Z  I  G  M  N  G  R  P  T  B  R  I
D  W  T  R  S  F  Z  L  T  D  K  R  I  N  J  I  R  Y  L  B
R  M  E  C  H  I  L  D  R  E  N  N  M  N  X  R  U  L  N  P
I  D  D  R  U  G  A  B  U  S  E  D  I  V  G  A  M  A  C  V
S  U  O  R  E  C  N  A  C  E  R  P  A  R  W  T  N  W  F  N
E  R  U  S  O  P  X  E  V  U  A  I  G  L  D  I  T  A  U  E
Q  M  F  P  N  O  E  N  P  W  U  J  F  U  Z  O  F  S  O  A
A  R  U  K  F  K  V  U  L  O  A  P  O  F  L  N  F  V  Y  S
G  Q  J  H  E  S  K  I  N  A  V  O  B  V  G  V  A  N  W
H  Z  U  N  C  P  H  M  D  X  E  O  C  S  U  Y  J  V  D  B
S  E  C  I  O  H  C  Y  R  A  T  E  I  D  R  O  O  P  W  A
```

Conditions And Disorders of the Skin

primary lesions

Match the primary lesions on the left to the descriptions on the right.

_____ **1.** tubercle

_____ **2.** macule

_____ **3.** cyst

_____ **4.** papule

_____ **5.** tumor

_____ **6.** vesicle

_____ **7.** wheal

_____ **8.** bulla

_____ **9.** pustule

A. large blister containing watery fluid

B. closed, fluid-filled mass below the surface of the skin

C. pimple; small skin swelling that sometimes contains pus

D. flat, discolored spot such as a freckle; flat rash

E. small blister or sac containing clear fluid

F. inflamed, pus-filled pimple

G. abnormal mass caused by excessive multiplication of cells

H. itchy, swollen lesion that lasts only a few hours

I. round, solid lump that can be above or below the skin; larger than a papule

secondary lesions

Match the secondary lesions at the left to the descriptions on the right.

_____ **1.** crust

_____ **2.** excoriation

_____ **3.** fissure

_____ **4.** scale

_____ **5.** scar or cicatrix

_____ **6.** ulcer

A. chapped hands

B. an open lesion on the skin

C. scratch

D. a mark on the skin formed after an injury

E. epidermal flakes, dry or oily, such as dandruff

F. dead cells that form over wounds while healing

skin conditions

Match the following skin conditions to the appropriate descriptions or definitions on the right.

_____ 1. albinism

_____ 2. lentigines

_____ 3. leukoderma

_____ 4. nevus

_____ 5. stain

_____ 6. tan

_____ 7. vitiligo

_____ 8. keloid

_____ 9. chloasma

_____ 10. mole

_____ 11. acne

_____ 12. fissure

_____ 13. hematoma

_____ 14. lesion

_____ 15. hypertrophy

A. caused by a burn or congenital disease

B. absence of melanin of the body; pink eyes

C. darkening of skin due to exposure to UV rays

D. birthmark; malformation due to dilated capillaries

E. milky-white spots

F. permanent brown or wine-colored skin discoloration

G. freckles

H. chronic inflammation of the sebaceous glands from retained secretions and bacteria.

I. increased pigmentation on the skin, in spots that are not elevated.

J. crack in the skin that penetrates the dermis.

K. collection of blood that is trapped underneath the nail.

L. abnormal growth of the skin

M. thick scar

N. mark on the skin

O. small brownish spot or blemish on the skin, ranging in color from pale tan to brown or bluish black.

Business Tip:

Understanding the structure and health of the skin will help you in choosing the right products and services for your clients. Skin health can be just as important to your clients as nail health and many will be willing to pay extra for it.

chapter 7: skin structure and growth

Complete the multiple-choice questions below by circling the correct answer to each question.

1. What percent of the body's weight is comprised of water?
   a. 40-60 percent
   b. 50-70 percent
   c. 60-80 percent
   d. 70-90 percent

2. What types of environmental issues, besides sun exposure, can lead to premature aging of the skin?
   a. Airborne pollutants
   b. Global warming
   c. Secondhand smoke
   d. A and C

3. Water aids in:
   a. The elimination of toxins and waste
   b. Regulating the body's temperature
   c. Proper digestion
   d. All of the above

4. _____ is an inflammatory, painful itching disease of the skin, presenting many forms of dry or moist lesions?
   a. Psoriasis
   b. Eczema
   c. Sun spots
   d. Moles

5. What is the largest organ of the body?
   a. Lungs
   b. Liver
   c. Intestines
   d. Skin

6. What is a non-contagious condition characterized by red patches covered with silver-white scales.
   a. Psoriasis
   b. Eczema
   c. Sun spots
   d. Moles

7. What happens to the skin as collagen and elastin fibers weaken with age?
   a. Darkens
   b. Sags
   c. Wrinkles
   d. Shows age spots

8. Nutrients carried to the skin include molecules of _____ derived from food.
   a. Protein and fats
   b. Vitamins
   c. Minerals
   d. All of the above

9. What percentage does heredity generally contribute to visible skin aging?
   a. 5%
   b. 10%
   c. 15%
   d. 30%

10. Psoriasis is typically found on the:
    a. Feet and hands
    b. Knees and elbows
    c. Chest and lower back
    d. B and C

11. What is the primary factor in skin aging?
    a. Smoking
    b. Photo-aging or sun exposure
    c. Car exhaust
    d. B and C

12. Moles that have undergone a change in _____, should be immediately checked by a dermatologist.
    a. Color
    b. Size
    c. Shape
    d. All of the above

13. What is the best defense against pollutants?
    a. A good daily skincare regimen.
    b. Taking vitamins
    c. Drinking water regularly
    d. B and C

14. What is a characteristic of healthy skin?
    a. Slightly moist and soft
    b. Hairy
    c. Pink
    d. All of the above

15. What is carried through the bloodstream to the skin?
    a. Oxygen
    b. Nutrients
    c. Water
    d. A and B

8 nail structure and growth

While your goal for nail school should be to learn how to expertly groom, strengthen, and beautify the nails, it is equally important to understand their physiology. You will be using these terms daily as a working nail technician and will likely be tested on these terms also!

nail structure key words puzzle

Fill in the crossword puzzle with key words found in chapter 8, by using the clues below.

ACROSS

1 All the anatomical parts of the fingernail necessary to produce the natural nail plate.

8 Hardened keratin plate covering the nail bed. It slowly slides across the nail bed while it grows.

10 Slightly thickened layer of skin that lies between the fingertip and free edge of the nail plate. It forms a protective barrier that prevents microorganisms from invading and infecting the nail bed.

11 Dead, colorless tissue that tightly adheres to the natural nail plate.

12 Area where the nail plate cells are formed; this area is composed of matrix cells that make up the nail plate.

DOWN

1 Portion of the living skin that supports the nail plate as it grows toward the free edge.

2 Fold of normal skin that surrounds the nail plate.

3 Whitish, half-moon shape at the base of the nail plate, caused by the reflection of light off the surface of the matrix.

4 Thin layer of tissue between the nail plate and the nail bed.

5 Slit or furrow on the sides of the nail.

6 Living skin at the base of the nail plate and covering the matrix area.

7 Part of the nail plate that extends over the tip of the finger or toe.

9 Tough bank of fibrous tissue that connects bones or holds an organ in place.

Nail Anatomy

label this!

Label the parts of the natural nail using the terms listed below.

Bone
Collagen fibers
Cuticle

Eponychium
Hyponychium
Nail bed

Nail plate
Proximal nail fold
Solehorn

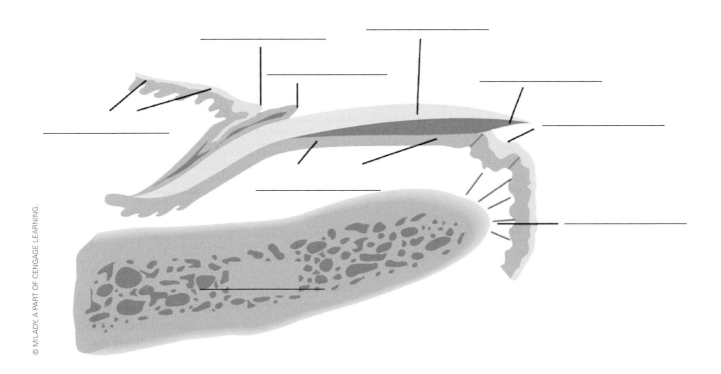

© MILADY, A PART OF CENGAGE LEARNING.

Fun Fact...

Fingernails grow nearly 4 times faster than toenails. Your middle fingernail grows the fastest.

Source: http://www.didyouknow.org/fastfacts/body.htm

chapter 8: nail structure and growth

Complete the multiple-choice questions below by circling the correct answer to each question.

1. What is the water content of a healthy nail?
   a. 10% to 20%
   b. 15% to 25%
   c. 20% to 30%
   d. 25% to 35%

2. What affects nail growth?
   a. Nutrition
   b. Exercise
   c. General health
   d. All of the above

3. What does a longer matrix produce?
   a. A thicker nail plate
   b. A thinner nail plate
   c. Larger lunula
   d. None of the above

4. After losing a toenail, how long does it take for a new nail to completely take its place?
   a. 5 months
   b. 7 months
   c. 9 months
   d. 12 months

5. How long does ordinary replacement of the natural nail take?
   a. 2 to 4 months
   b. 4 to 6 months
   c. 6 to 8 months
   d. None of the above

6. What are nails made out of?
   a. Minerals
   b. Keratin
   c. Cartilage
   d. None of the above

7. What does a healthy nail look like?
   a. Whitish
   b. Yellowish
   c. Translucent
   d. A and C

8. What does an adequate amount of water do for the nail?
   a. Makes it thick
   b. Makes it flexible
   c. Makes it brittle
   d. Makes it yellowish

9. What does an inadequate amount of water cause?
   a. Thinness
   b. Yellowish
   c. Rigidity
   d. Whitish

10. Poor nail growth is caused by what factors?
    a. Poor general health
    b. Injury to the matrix
    c. Nail disorder or disease
    d. All of the above

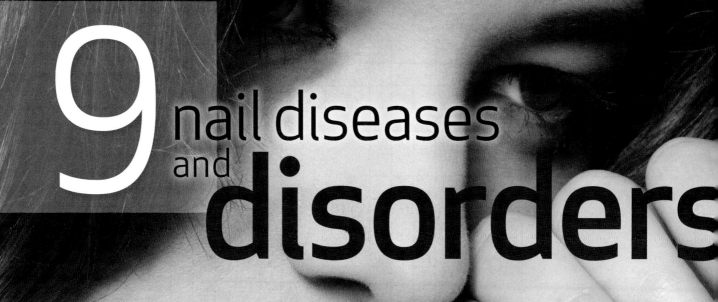

9 nail diseases and disorders

While reviewing this chapter you will begin to recognize the disorders and diseases that can affect the nails of hands and feet. This, in turn, will give you the professional knowledge you will need to know when it is safe to work on a client! This chapter is very important, not only because these terms may be on your school and licensing exams, but because for the rest of your professional life as a nail technician, you will be approached by friends, family, and clients about nail disorders they are experiencing.

Knowing your business sets you apart as a professional!

understanding nail disorders puzzle

Complete the crossword puzzle below by naming the nail disorders using the clues given.

ACROSS

1 Bitten nails.

3 Redness, pain, swelling, or pus; refer to physician.

5 Darkening of the fingernails or toenails.

9 Abnormal stretching of skin around the nail plate; usually from serious injury or an allergic skin reaction.

13 Nails turn variety of colors; may indicate surface staining, a systemic disorder, poor blood circulation.

14 Noticeably thin, white plate, more flexible than normal; usually caused by improper diet, hereditary factors, internal disease, or medication.

15 A form of dramatically increased nail curvature.

16 Nail surface pitting, roughness, onycholysis, and bed discolorations.

DOWN

2 Sharp bend in one corner of the nail plate creating increased curvature.

4 Depressions running across the width of the nail plate; a result of serious illness or injury.

6 Whitish discoloration of the nails; usually caused by minor injury to the nail matrix. Not related to health.

7 Lengthwise, wavy ridges seen in normal aging.

8 Dark purplish spots, usually due to injury.

10 Abnormal surface roughness on the nail plate.

11 Living skin around the nail plate (often the eponychium) becomes split or torn.

12 A form of dramatically increased nail curvature.

recognizing nail diseases

Label the following photos with the name of the nail disease or disorder.

1. _____

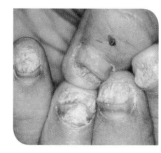

COURTESY OF ROBERT BARAN, M.D. (FRANCE)

2. _____

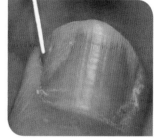

COURTESY OF ROBERT BARAN, M.D. (FRANCE)

3. _____

© MILADY, A PART OF CENGAGE LEARNING.

4. _____

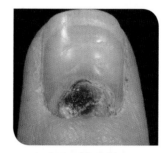

REPRINTED WITH PERMISSION FROM AMERICAN ACADEMY OF DERMATOLOGY. ALL RIGHTS RESERVED.

5. _____

COURTESY OF ROBERT BARAN, M.D. (FRANCE)

Fun **Fact...**

Certain health problems in the body can show up in the nails as visible disorders or poor nail growth.

chapter 9: nail diseases and disorders

Complete the multiple-choice questions below by circling the correct answer to each question.

1. A condition caused by an injury or disease of the nail unit is called:
   a. Onychosis
   b. A nail disorder
   c. Onycholysis
   d. Onychia

2. What nail disease causes the separation and falling off of a nail plate from the bed?
   a. Onychosis
   b. Onychomadesis
   c. Onychomycosis
   d. Onychia

3. Any nail disease that shows signs of infection or inflammation (redness, pain, swelling, or pus) should:
   a. Be carefully serviced to not break the skin
   b. Only manicured, artificial products should not be applied.
   c. Not be diagnosed or treated in the salon
   d. Not be soaked in water or other solutions

4. A normal healthy nail appears:
   a. Firm and flexible
   b. Shiny
   c. Slightly pink in color
   d. All of the above

5. Clients with yellow, green, brown, or black spots on their nails should:
   a. Remove nail enhancements immediately
   b. Be immediately referred to a physician for treatment
   c. Receive nail bleaching treatments
   d. A and B

6. Onychomycosis is
   a. A fungal infection of the nail plate
   b. An ingrown toenail
   c. Inflammation of the nail matrix
   d. Discoloring of the nail

7. Onychocryptosis is referred to as:
   a. Black nails
   b. Green nails
   c. Ingrown nails
   d. Bitten nails

8. Onychia is an inflammation of the nail matrix followed by:
   a. Bruising of the nail bed
   b. Shedding of the natural nail plate
   c. Pus surrounding cuticle
   d. Beau's lines

9. Pseudomonas aeruginosa is one of several common _____ that can cause nail infection.
   a. Diseases
   b. Bacteria
   c. Fungi
   d. Virus

10. Any deformity or disease of the natural nails is called:
    a. Onychosis
    b. A nail disorder
    c. Onycholysis
    d. Onychia

11. What nail condition is easily treated in the salon?
    a. Hangnails
    b. A bruise on the nail bed
    c. A dark green spot
    d. A and B

12. A typical bacterial infection on the nail plate can be identified in the early stages as:
    a. A yellow-green spot
    b. Splitting nail
    c. White spots
    d. B and C

13. Infections can be caused by:
    a. Moisture trapped under a nail enhancement
    b. Large numbers of bacteria or fungal organisms on a surface
    c. Oil on the nail plate
    d. A and B

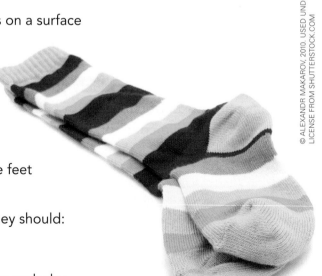

14. If a client has tinea pedis, he should be advised to:
    a. Wash and dry feet completely everyday
    b. Change cotton socks twice a day
    c. Use over the counter antifungal powder on the feet
    d. All of the above

15. If a client is susceptible to paronychia infections they should:
    a. Use hand lotions to keep skin healthy.
    b. Keep feet dry and clean.
    c. Soak their hands or feet in water for 30 minutes each day.
    d. A and B

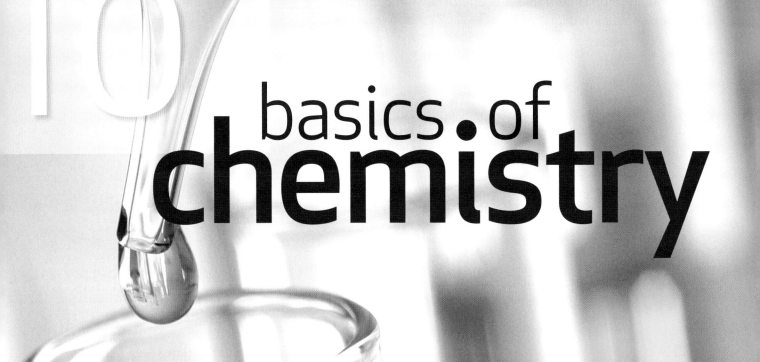

basics.of chemistry

To use professional products effectively and safely, all nail professionals need to have a basic understanding of chemistry. With this knowledge you can trouble-shoot and solve common problems with nail services.

basic chemistry puzzle

Complete the crossword puzzle below with keywords found in Chapter 10 by using the clues on the following page.

ACROSS

5 Special types of ingredients used in nail polish dryers and skin protectants.
9 A mixture of two or more immiscible substances united with the aid of a binder or emulsifier.
14 The substance that is dissolved in a solution.
16 Those characteristics that can only be determined by a chemical reaction and a chemical change in the substance.
19 A measure of the acidity or alkalinity of a substance.
22 The smallest particle of an element that still retains the properties of that element.
23 A change in the chemical and physical properties of a substance by a chemical reaction that creates a new substance or substances.
25 An unstable mixture of undissolved particles in a liquid.
26 Easily evaporating.
27 The simplest form of matter, which cannot be broken down into a simpler substance without a loss of identity.
28 Surface active agents; substances that act as a bridge to allow oil and water to mix, or emulsify.

DOWN

1 Combinations of two or more atoms of different elements united together chemically.
2 Those characteristics that can be determined without a chemical reaction and that do not cause a chemical change in the substance.
3 Oil loving.
4 Substances containing carbon which evaporate quickly and easily.
6 Not capable of being mixed.
7 Capable of being mixed with another liquid in any proportion without separating.
8 Two or more atoms joined chemically.
10 A stable mixture of two or more mixable substances.
11 Water loving.
12 A change in the form or physical properties of a substance without the formation of a new substance.
13 Chemical combinations of atoms of the same element.
15 A physical combination of matter, in any proportions.
17 Chemical reactions which produce heat.
18 Science that deals with the composition, structures, and properties of matter, and how matter changes under different conditions.
20 A chemical combination of matter, in definite proportions.
21 Sweet, colorless, oily substance used as a moisturizing ingredient in cosmetic products.
24 The substance that dissolves the solute to form a solution.

Chemistry

fact or fiction

Answer true or false to the following statements.

T   F   **1.** A stable mixture of two or more mixable substances is called an emulsion.

T   F   **2.** A common example of suspension is oil-and-vinegar salad dressing.

T   F   **3.** Matter exists in three forms.

T   F   **4.** Solid matter has shape and no volume.

T   F   **5.** Liquid matter does not have a shape or volume.

T   F   **6.** Depending on its temperature, matter can change forms.

T   F   **7.** Because hydroxide ions are alkaline, they influence the alkalinity of water.

T   F   **8.** Only products that contain oil can have a pH.

T   F   **9.** The pH of any substance is always a balance of both acidity and alkalinity.

T   F   **10.** Pure water is 40 % acid and 60 % alkaline.

chapter 10: basics of chemistry

Complete the multiple-choice questions below by circling the correct answer to each question.

1. The branch of chemistry dealing with compounds lacking carbon, such as minerals, water, and metals is called:
   a. Organic chemistry
   b. Inorganic chemistry
   c. Compound chemistry
   d. None of the above

2. An atom or molecule that carries an electrical charge is called:
   a. A molecule
   b. Matter
   c. An ion
   d. Atoms

Fun Fact...

The word "atom" comes from the Greek word atomos, meaning "uncut" or "that which can't be split."

Source: http://education.jlab.org/qa/history

3. What causes an atom or molecule to split in two, creating a pair of ions with opposite electrical charges?
   a. Ionization
   b. Mitosis
   c. Magnetic change
   d. Atomic division

4. An ion with a negative electrical charge is called a/an:
   a. Cation
   b. Suspension
   c. Anion
   d. None of the above

5. A/an _____ is an ion with a positive electrical charge.
   a. Anion
   b. Cation
   c. Solute
   d. Suspension

6. When two or more atoms are joined together, they form what?
   a. Matter
   b. A molecule
   c. Space
   d. Solvent

7. All matter has physical properties that we can:
   a. Touch
   b. Smell
   c. See
   d. All of the above

8. How many naturally occurring elements are there?

    a. 60

    b. 70

    c. 80

    d. 90

9. All living things, whether they are plant or animal, contain what?

    a. Minerals

    b. pH

    c. Water

    d. Carbon

10. Any substance that occupies space is called

    a. Present

    b. Matter

    c. Cells

    d. None of the above

11. What ways can matter be changed?

    a. Emotionally

    b. Physically

    c. Chemically

    d. B and C

12. The pH scale goes from _____, with 7 being neutral.

    a. 1-14

    b. 0-14

    c. 1-15

    d. 0-7

13. Below 7 on the pH scale, the solution is:

    a. Solvent

    b. Acidic

    c. Alkaline

    d. None of the above

14. Hair and skin have an average pH of:

    a. 3

    b. 5

    c. 7

    d. 9

15. Physical mixtures that contain two or more different substances are called:

    a. Solutions

    b. Suspensions

    c. Emulsions

    d. All of the above

11

nail product
chemistry
SIMPLIFIED

Your knowledge of the chemistry in the nail products you use will give you a great advantage—you'll be able to troubleshoot and solve many common problems that can cause service breakdown and problem nails for your clients. Chemical knowledge is the key to becoming a great nail professional. Even if you just want to "do nails," your success depends on having an understanding of chemicals and chemistry.

understanding chemicals

Fill in the term for each clue and then find the word in the word find puzzle on the next page.

_____ **1.** Ingredients used to keep nail enhancement products flexible

_____ **2.** Ingredients which control color stability and prevent sunlight from causing fading or discoloration.

_____ **3.** Chemical reaction resulting in two surfaces sticking together.

_____ **4.** The name for an entire family of chemicals used to make all types of nail enhancements and adhesives.

_____ **5.** Products that cover the nail plate with a hard film.

_____ **6.** A substance capable of seriously damaging skin, eyes, or other soft tissues on contact.

_____ **7.** Monomer that joins together different polymer chains.

_____ **8.** A state of matter different from a liquid or solid.

_____ **9.** A type of acrylic monomer (crosslinking) that has very good adhesion to the natural nail plate and polymerizes in minutes.

_____ **10.** Dangerously prolonged, repeated, or long-term contact with certain chemicals.

_____ **11.** Chemical reaction that creates polymers, also called curing or hardening.

_____ **12.** Individual molecule that joins others of its kind to make a polymer.

_____ **13.** A specialized acrylic monomer (crosslinking) that has good adhesion to the natural nail plate and polymerizes in minutes.

_____ **14.** Short monomer chain that has had its chain growth halted before it became a polymer.

_____ **15.** A specialized acrylic monomer (non-crosslinking) that has excellent adhesion to the natural nail plate and polymerizes in seconds.

_____ **16.** Change from liquid to vapor form.

_____ **17.** What is formed when liquids evaporate into the air.

_____ **18.** Substances that speed up chemical reactions.

_____ **19.** Substance formed by combining many small molecules (monomers) or oligomers, usually in an extremely long, chain-like structure.

```
N P E X O L C Y A N O A C R Y L A T E P
Z O Q V Z S S C S V K M S K Y P O I L O
X W I B A M G W I S L E A Y C L Y A V V
R L J T L P H N Q L T D N O I B S Y K E
G A S G A O O D I A Y O A G A T E Q X R
A N A K V Z F R L T I R O X I I T Q I E
A V Y H S B I Y A S A M C C I M A C O X
U U P F X G R R E T E O I A O C L J W P
I V G B P C X H E R E Z C N L Y Y R N O
C R S W A I D X T M E Z O B Q A R E Q S
Q B J T R A E W W R Y M J Q C N C R E U
D R T N A Q V N S Z E L K F C M A X I R
R O P A V B U C D R O M O Z O P H X G E
O O Y C K B I S N L M A U P R O T H H X
Q I Q R A H Q L F B H G P L R L E A W V
T C T C L X C Y I P N B X N O Y M V F H
C A T A L Y S T S Z Y C E J S M Y O N O
A L U E F E B B Q V E N V K I E U G B L
R E K N I L S S O R C R R P V R Z X T J
H P B L D U K Y P F D Y S B E I K J G W
```

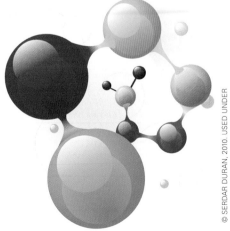

salon chemistry mini quiz

Answer these questions about product chemistry and how it works in the salon.

1. What two factors ensure good adhesion?

_____

_____

_____

2. How can the risk of fingernail infections be minimized in the salon?

_____

_____

_____

3. How do you remove surface shine from the nail?

_____

_____

_____

4. Why is it better to only dehydrate one hand at a time?

_____

_____

_____

5. Explain how the condition of the natural nail plate plays a role in a nail enhancement's strength.

_____

_____

_____

6. What are the two main types of nail coatings and how do they work?

_____

_____

_____

7. What is methyl methacrylate monomer (MMA) used for?

_____

_____

_____

8. What should you do if your clients are having problems with their nail enhancements lifting?

_____

_____

_____

9. When nail problems do arise, what are the most likely culprits?

_____

_____

_____

10. Why should you put a towel over your client's hands when removing nail enhancements by soaking the fingertips in acetone?

_____

_____

_____

Fun **Fact...**

Everything you can see or touch, except light or electricity is a chemical.

chapter 11: nail product chemistry simplified

Complete the multiple-choice questions below by circling the correct answer to each question.

1. What is an example of a methacrylate?
   a. Nail adhesives
   b. Monomer liquids
   c. Monomer powders
   d. B and C

2. What is an example of an acrylate?
   a. Monomer liquids
   b. Monomer powders
   c. UV gels
   d. A and B

3. What is an example of a cyanoacrylate?
   a. Nail adhesives
   b. UV gels
   c. Nail wrap resin
   d. A and C

4. What is an example of a nail coating?
   a. Nail polish
   b. UV gel
   c. Nail wrap resins
   d. All of the above

5. Why do many nail salons not use MMA nail enhancement products?
   a. It can cause a lot of damage to the natural nail when removing.
   b. It is dangerous to inhale.
   c. It is a carcinogen
   d. All of the above

6. An example of a corrosive nail product is:
   a. Primer
   b. UV Gel
   c. Polymer
   d. Adhesive

7. Before a nail coating is applied, the first step to prep the nails should be:
   a. Remove shine with a medium/fine (240 grit) abrasive or buffer
   b. Use a nail dehydrator
   c. Wash and scrub hands and nails
   d. Use a hand sanitizer

8. Which of the following is used to make all liquid/powder systems and at least one type of UV gel:
   a. Methacrylate
   b. Methyl methacrylate monomer
   c. Cyanoacrylate
   d. None of the above

9. What can interfere with product adhesion?
   a. Irregular shaped nail plate
   b. Surface oils and contaminants
   c. Client's age
   d. A and B

10. What types of products form vapors?
    a. Water, alcohol, and acetone
    b. UV gels, wrap resins, and adhesives
    c. Candles, incense, and cigarettes
    d. A and B

what would you do? a salon **scenario**

You've been working at Tip-to-Toe nail salon for over a year and have never had any allergy to your products, but all of a sudden you have broken out in a rash on the underside of your right forearm. Your dermatologist says that you are experiencing a skin allergy that is probably from overexposure to your nail enhancement products. You can't stop working, so what can you do?

_____

_____

_____

_____

_____

_____

_____

_____

_____

12 basics of electricity

Understanding the basics of electricity will help you to avoid injury and fire and help to keep you, your clients, and the salon safe! Let's begin.

electrical terms double puzzle!

Unscramble the key terms listed below using the clues given and write the word inside the cells. Copy the letters in the numbered cells to the other cells with the same number to reveal the secret message!

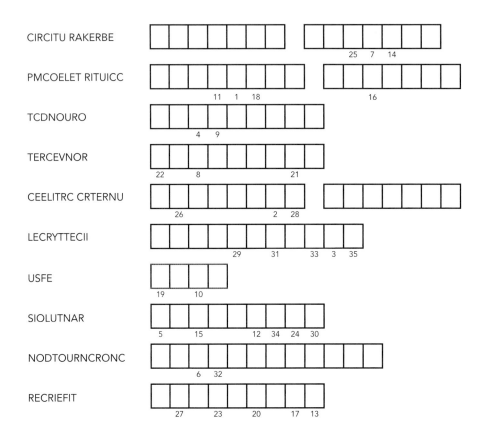

CIRCITU RAKERBE — 25 7 14

PMCOELET RITUICC — 11 1 18 — 16

TCDNOURO — 4 9

TERCEVNOR — 22 8 21

CEELITRC CRTERNU — 26 2 28

LECRYTTECII — 29 31 33 3 35

USFE — 19 10

SIOLUTNAR — 5 15 12 34 24 30

NODTOURNCRONC — 6 32

RECRIEFIT — 27 23 20 17 13

Clues

1 Switch that automatically interrupts or shuts off an electric circuit at the first indication of overload.

2 The path of an electric current from the generating source through conductors and back to its original source.

3 Any substance that conducts electricity.

4 Apparatus that changes direct current to alternating current.

5 Flow of electricity along a conductor.

6 Movement of particles around an atom that creates pure energy.

7 Special device that prevents excessive current from passing through a circuit.

8 Substance that does not easily transmit electricity.

9 Not a conductor.

10 Apparatus that changes alternating current to direct current.

Secret Message:

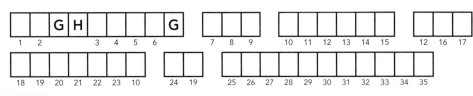

G H — G
1 2 — 3 4 5 6 — 7 8 9 — 10 11 12 13 14 15 — 12 16 17
18 19 20 21 22 23 10 — 24 19 — 25 26 27 28 29 30 31 32 33 34 35

Fun Fact...

Thomas Edison invented the first long-lasting light bulb and owned the first power plant ever! The power plant was opened in New York City in 1882. Today, one power plant can make enough electricity for 188,000 homes.

Source: http://library.thinkquest.org/06aug/00442/whatsupelectricity.html

Electricity
need to know!

Identify and describe these important acronyms about electrical measurements and types of electrical current.

1. AC – _____

_____

2. DC – _____

_____

3. K – _____

_____

4. O – _____

_____

5. UV light – _____

_____

6. V – _____

_____

7. W – _____

_____

8. A – _____

_____

_____

Fun Fact...

Just as a water hose must be able to expand as the amount of water flowing through it increases, so a wire must expand with an increase in the amount of electrons (amps). A hair dryer rated at 12 amps must have a cord that is twice as thick as one rated at 5 amps; otherwise, the cord might overheat and start a fire.

Electrical Equipment Safety

safe use of electrical equipment

Circle true or false about the following statements on the safe use of electrical equipment.

T   F   **1.** Keep all wires, plugs, and electrical equipment in good repair.

T   F   **2.** Do not leave your client for more than 10 minutes while connected to an electrical device.

T   F   **3.** All the electrical appliances you use should be DC certified.

T   F   **4.** Be careful when cleaning around electric outlets while equipment is plugged in.

T   F   **5.** Do not touch two metal objects at the same time if either is connected to an electric current.

T   F   **6.** Do not step on or place objects on electrical cords.

T   F   **7.** Read all instructions carefully before using any piece of electrical equipment.

T   F   **8.** Disconnect appliances by pulling on the cord, not the plug.

T   F   **9.** Disconnect all appliances when not in use.

T   F   **10.** Inspect all electrical equipment once a year.

T   F   **11.** Use a power strip when there are many plugs for one outlet.

T   F   **12.** You and your client should avoid contact with water and metal surfaces when using electricity, and do not handle electrical equipment with wet hands.

T   F   **13.** Keep all electrical cords off the floor and away from people's feet; getting tangled in a cord could cause you or your client to trip.

T   F   **14.** Do not allow electrical cords to become twisted; this can cause a short circuit.

T   F   **15.** Salon staff should only try to repair electrical appliances when they are unplugged.

chapter 12: basics of electricity

Complete the multiple-choice questions below by circling the correct answer to each question.

1. Current will not flow through a conductor unless the _____ is/are stronger than the resistance (ohms).
   a. Force, volts
   b. Ampere, amps
   c. Watts
   d. UV light

2. What does wattage tell you about UV nail lamp bulbs?
   a. How bright a light bulb is
   b. How much electricity it consumes during use
   c. How powerful the light bulb is
   d. A and C

3. What type of electrical plug offers the most protection for you and your client?
   a. One with two rectangular prongs
   b. One with two rectangular prongs where one is slightly larger than the other
   c. One with two rectangular prongs and a third circular ground
   d. None of the above

4. What is in ordinary water that makes it a good conductor of electricity?
   a. Copper
   b. Ions
   c. Minerals
   d. Acid

5. What material makes a good insulator?
   a. Silk
   b. Wood
   c. Cement
   d. All of the above

Part3

NAIL CARE

13
manicuring

Welcome to manicuring! The manicure is the foundation for all of the services you will perform in your nail technology career. The implements and tools you will use in the basic manicure will be the same implements and tools you'll use on almost every client that ever sits at your table. The skills you'll hone in this chapter will be the basis for all you will be able to do in your career—so get ready to take notes and practice!

manicure key words puzzle

Fill in the crossword puzzle with key words found in chapter 13, by using the clues below.

ACROSS

4 The list of services that you are legally allowed to perform in your specialty in your state.

7 The act of causing tiny unseen openings in the skin that may allow entry by pathogenic microbes.

8 Designed to absorb into the nail plate to increase flexibility, and into the surrounding skin to soften.

9 A hardener that adds cross-links to the natural nail plate, but unlike those containing formaldehyde, DMU does not cause adverse skin reactions.

10 Implements that are generally stainless steel as they must be properly cleaned and disinfected prior to use on another client.

11 Involves the use of highly concentrated, non-oily, and volatile essential oils to induce such reactions as relaxation, invigoration or to simply create a pleasant fragrance during the service.

12 A succession of strokes by gliding the hands over an area of the body with varying degrees of pressure or contact.

13 The manipulation of the soft tissues of the body.

14 Oils extracted using various forms of distillation from seeds, bark, roots, leaves, wood, and/or resin.

DOWN

1 A petroleum by-product that has excellent sealing properties (barrier qualities) to hold the moisture in the skin.

2 Implements that cannot be reused and must be thrown away after a single use.

3 Sets of all the tools that will be used in a service to the nail, or to apply products

5 A combination of clear polish and protein, such as collagen.

6 Barrier products that contain ingredients designed to seal the surface and hold in the subdermal moisture in the skin.

Manicuring

tools of the trade

Fill in the blanks below with the correct term using the clues provided. Then find the term in the word find puzzle on the following page.

_____ **1.** Tools used to perform nail services that are multiple use (re-useable) or disposable.

_____ **2.** A wooden stick used to remove cuticle tissue from the nail plate (by gently pushing), to clean under the free edge of the nail.

_____ **3.** Boards and buffers less than 180 grit that quickly reduce the thickness of any surface.

_____ **4.** A multi-use implement made of stainless steel; used to push back the eponychium, but can also be used to gently scrape cuticle tissue from the natural nail plate.

_____ **5.** 240 grit and higher abrasives designed for buffing, polishing, and removing very fine scratches.

_____ **6.** A stainless steel implement used to carefully trim away dead skin around the nails.

_____ **7.** A multi-use implement used to shorten the nail plate quickly and efficiently.

_____ **8.** 180 to 240 grit abrasives that are used to smooth and refine surfaces and shorten natural nails.

_____ **9.** For soaking the client's fingers in warm water to soften the skin and cuticle.

_____ **10.** Needed for lighting the work area.

_____ **11.** The surface on which the manicurist works.

_____ **12.** Worn to protect the nail technician from exposure to microbes during services.

_____ **13.** Container that holds implements to be disinfected.

_____ **14.** For cushioning the client's arm when performing nail services.

_____ **15.** Used for moisturization of the skin and can be added to manicures and pedicures for an extra charge.

```
L Q R P W I R P R Z F P N W W U L N Y M A M F N M
N O A E L O E E F E A V P H J H W I Y A D E I A Q
F B W W N H O P H R P L D G N K P M K N J D N I W
G I O E A I V D A S H P Z N E Y Y P C I U I E L J
G V N F R R A F E S U Q I I Z F K L T C S U G C W
C L Z G I G F T F N E P Z N A K Y E O U T M R L U
Y I O W E I R V N K P L L K B J O M X R A G I I V
G S K V N R T I I O Z U I A C H N E N E B R T P C
C R M B E Y B R T A C M S V T O K N V T L I A P E
U V A Z X S K O S A J N Z H I E P T V A E T B E V
Z T R C I D K J W F B L O H E U M S I B L A R R Z
H O T Y A D B J A L L R S I P R L A G L A B A S A
T H U L S F D J E G V U A C T Y N Q D E M R S Y J
P Z F F N H P S I V C B G S D C H E M C P A I Y U
D X Q Y I F Z F Y M Q C W D I S E E Y I H S V O Y
G Z A B O F G V R E C R M J W V K F I X L I E P O
H F T Z P D U A N E D W I X O Q E X N Q D V S W P
R Y D G T T U R K M I Y D E Z Y S L I I E N S I
R Y G I Z N I P G L G U V M A E U N O B S S H V M
G K P I E Q U E Q W W R D N R I E J G F T I J O Z
U L C I F T Y L O N D N S L W H W P P V I L D U J
N P L H Y V B F W K G T X L Y S J J T W M P L R H
L C G N M F H R O P N B K I U X W C G U W O S V K
Z T K E P M Q E R G R S Q V R O K N R N C E Z Y U
K N V V I W Z E F V M X T G H H F B K V F J V S I
```

cleaning up!

Write in the 7 step numbers to show the correct cleaning and disinfection procedure for nail implements and tools.

Step _____   Rinse all implements with warm running water.

Step _____   Thoroughly wash them with soap, a nail brush, and warm water. Brush grooved items, if necessary, and open hinged implements to scrub the area.

Step _____   Immerse cleansed implements in an appropriate disinfection container holding an EPA-registered disinfectant for the required time (usually 10 minutes).

Step _____   Put on gloves.

Step _____   Rinse away all traces of soap on implements with warm running water.

Step _____ Remove gloves and thoroughly wash your hands with liquid soap, rinse, and dry with a clean fabric or disposable towel.

Step _____ Dry implements thoroughly with a clean or disposable towel, or allow to air dry on a clean towel.

Manicuring

draw this manicure table set up!

Draw the following manicure supplies in the correct place on the manicure table below. Mark the products with the correlating letter.

Tech Tip:

Some of the products belong inside the drawer.

A. Arm cushion wrapped
B. Terrycloth towel or disposable towel
C. Disinfectant container
D. Implements
E. Cuticle remover

F. Abrasives and buffers
G. Fingerbowl with warm water
H. Hand lotions or creams
I. Manicure brush
J. Plastic bag

K. Colored polish
L. Cotton balls
M. Polish remover
N. Clean and disinfected implements in an unsealed container

Manicure Table Set-Up ▼

drawer ▶

nail shapes word scramble

Unscramble the five basic nail shapes using the clues given below.

lvao ailn   undro anli   vuslaqo nlia
noiedpt lian   qraseu alin

1. _____ A nail completely straight across the free edge with no rounding at the outside edges.

2. _____ A nail with a square free edge that is rounded off at the corner edges.

3. _____ A slightly tapered nail, usually extends just a bit past the fingertip.

4. _____ Suited to thin hands with long fingers and narrow nail beds. The nail is tapered and longer than usual to emphasize and enhance the slender appearance of the hand.

5. _____ A conservative nail shape that is thought to be attractive on most women's hands. It is similar to a squoval nail with even more rounded corners.

Fun Fact...

Healthy nails grow about 2 cm each year. Fingernails grow four times as fast as toenails.

Source: http://biotech-uria.synthasite.com/fun-facts.php

exposure incident facts

Answer true or false to the following statements about what to do if you accidentally draw blood during a nail service.

T   F   **1.** Immediately put on gloves and inform your client of what has occurred. Apologize and proceed.

T   F   **2.** Apply slight pressure to the area with cotton to stop the bleeding.

T   F   **3.** Clean wound with alcohol.

T   F   **4.** Apply petroleum jelly to completely cover the wound

T   F   **5.** Complete the service, but avoid contact to the cut finger..

T   F   **6.** Clean and disinfect workstation, as necessary.

T   F   **7.** Discard all disposable contaminated objects such as wipes or cotton balls directly in the trash.

T   F   **8.** Deposit sharp disposables in the trash.

T   F   **9.** Before removing your gloves, all tools and implements that have come into contact with blood or body fluids must be thoroughly cleaned and completely immersed in an EPA-registered hospital disinfectant solution or 10 percent bleach solution for ten minutes. Because blood can carry pathogens, you should never touch an open sore or wound.

T   F   **10.** Wash your hands with soap and warm water before returning to the service.

Manicure Procedure

label this!

Describe what is happening in the photos of the manicure procedure below.

© MILADY, A PART OF CENGAGE LEARNING. PHOTOGRAPHY BY DINO PETROCELLI.

_____
_____
_____
_____
_____
_____

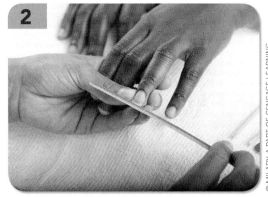

© MILADY, A PART OF CENGAGE LEARNING. PHOTOGRAPHY BY DINO PETROCELLI.

_____
_____
_____
_____
_____
_____

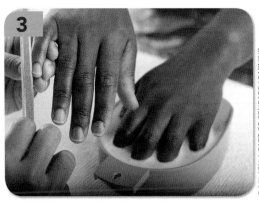

© MILADY, A PART OF CENGAGE LEARNING. PHOTOGRAPHY BY DINO PETROCELLI.

_____
_____
_____
_____
_____
_____

© MILADY, A PART OF CENGAGE LEARNING. PHOTOGRAPHY BY DINO PETROCELLI.

_____
_____
_____
_____
_____
_____

© MILADY, A PART OF CENGAGE LEARNING.
PHOTOGRAPHY BY DINO PETROCELLI.

© MILADY, A PART OF CENGAGE LEARNING.
PHOTOGRAPHY BY DINO PETROCELLI.

_____
_____
_____
_____
_____
_____

© MILADY, A PART OF CENGAGE LEARNING.
PHOTOGRAPHY BY DINO PETROCELLI.

© MILADY, A PART OF CENGAGE LEARNING.
PHOTOGRAPHY BY DINO PETROCELLI.

_____
_____
_____
_____
_____
_____

© MILADY, A PART OF CENGAGE LEARNING. PHOTOGRAPHY BY DINO PETROCELLI.

_____
_____
_____
_____
_____
_____
_____

© MILADY, A PART OF CENGAGE LEARNING. PHOTOGRAPHY BY DINO PETROCELLI.

_____
_____
_____
_____
_____
_____
_____

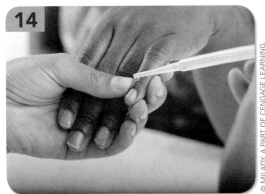

© MILADY, A PART OF CENGAGE LEARNING. PHOTOGRAPHY BY DINO PETROCELLI.

_____
_____
_____
_____
_____
_____
_____

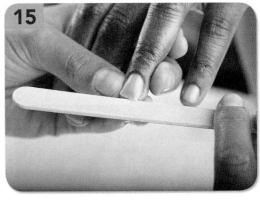

© MILADY, A PART OF CENGAGE LEARNING. PHOTOGRAPHY BY DINO PETROCELLI.

_____
_____
_____
_____
_____
_____
_____

16

_____

_____

_____

_____

_____

_____

17

_____

_____

_____

_____

_____

_____

polish application

Fill in the blanks with words or phrases to complete the statements about the proper technique for the application of nail polish.

1. Be certain the client's nail plates are clean of _____ and other _____.

2. Apply a thin coat of _____ to cover the entire nail plate of all nails.

3. When applying nail polish, remove the brush from the bottle and _____ the side of the brush _____ on the inside of the lip of the bottle to remove excess polish. You should have a _____ on the end of the other side of the brush large enough to apply _____ to the entire nail plate without having to re-dip the brush. Hold the brush at approximately a _____ angle.

4. Place the tip of the brush on the nail _____ away from the cuticle area in the _____ of the nail. Slightly _____ the brush onto the _____, producing a slight _____, ensuring the polish and brush do not touch the _____. _____ the brush toward the free edge of the nail, down the center.

5. Move to each side of the nail and _____ in even strokes towards the _____.

6. After finishing the first coat of each nail, move the brush back and forth on the _____, barely touching, to apply color to it. Use the same technique for every nail while applying the first coat of color.

7. When you return to apply the second coat, _____, just start at the base of the polish curve and move towards the free edge.

8. Apply _____ top coat to _____ and to give nails a _____, _____ appearance. Be sure to coat the _____ of the nail with top coat as well.

© MILADY, A PART OF CENGAGE LEARNING. PHOTOGRAPHY BY DINO PETROCELLI.

© MILADY, A PART OF CENGAGE LEARNING. PHOTOGRAPHY BY DINO PETROCELLI.

mini quiz: manicure upgrades

Answer the questions below in the space provided about manicure upgrades.

Why is a spa manicure more expensive and need a longer service time?

_____

_____

_____

_____

How and why would you incorporate aromatherapy in a manicuring service?

_____

_____

_____

© NANKA (KUCHERENKO OLENA), 2010. USED UNDER LICENSE FROM SHUTTERSTOCK.COM

Why would your client want to upgrade her manicure by adding a paraffin wax treatment?

_____

_____

_____

Why and when would you offer nail art during a manicure?

_____

_____

_____

_____

State Board Prep

manicuring mistakes

You've reviewed how the products are set on the table and what the procedure steps are, but there is still much more to remember for your state board exam. Answer Yes or No to these questions about common mistakes that can be made during the practical exam.

_____ 1. Should you let your fingers come in contact with the solution when removing implements from the disinfectant solution?

_____ 2. Should you spray off implements with water after they have been removed from your disinfectant solution and then dry them?

_____ 3. Should you place contaminated implements back onto your work table and/or in the drawer?

_____ 4. Should you clean and disinfect the work area (table) before beginning your exam?

_____ 5. Should you wash your hands before the exam and when necessary during the exam?

_____ 6. Should you have your models wash their hands and nails?

_____ 7. Should you replace caps on containers when not in use?

_____ 8. Should all products and containers be labeled by hand if not with a manufacturer label?

_____ 9. Should metal implements be completely immersed in disinfectant solution?

_____ 10. Should a disposable/clean towel be placed on the model's chair.

State Board Manicure Practice Exam

Find two students to partner with. Practice your state board manicure from table set up to polish on your "student model." During the process, have your "student examiner" check yes or no to the questions on the following page.

State Board Manicure Practical Exam

manicure procedure and table set-up

	YES	NO
1. Did the participant wash his or her hands before beginning the table setup?	☐	☐
2. Was the manicuring table properly cleaned and disinfected?	☐	☐
3. Was the model's chair/stool properly cleaned and disinfected?	☐	☐
4. Was a towel placed on the model's chair?	☐	☐
5. Was the arm/hand rest correctly prepared?	☐	☐
6. Was a clean towel placed across the table?	☐	☐
7. Was a labeled bag for contaminated items taped to the table?	☐	☐
8. Was a labeled trash bag taped to the table?	☐	☐
9. Did all products and containers have the manufacturer's or hand written labels?	☐	☐
10. Were all required supplies, implements, and equipment set up correctly?	☐	☐
11. Were all required implements placed in an approved disinfectant solution?	☐	☐
12. Were implements removed from the disinfectant in a sanitary manner?	☐	☐
13. Were implements sprayed with water and dried before use if immersed in a disinfectant?	☐	☐

filing

	YES	NO
14. Were the nails filed correctly from corners to center?	☐	☐
15. Was filing on top of the nail avoided?	☐	☐
16. Were the sidewalls of the fingers protected while filing?	☐	☐
17. Was the correct type of abrasive board used?	☐	☐
18. Was the shape of the nails consistent?	☐	☐
19. Was filing kept free from the cuticle area to avoid cuticle damage?	☐	☐
20. Were the finished nails smooth with no ragged edges?	☐	☐

cuticle

	YES	NO
21. Was the cuticle remover applied to the nails in a sanitary manner?	☐	☐
22. Were all implements properly held and manipulated?	☐	☐
23. Was the cuticle area kept free from damage?	☐	☐
24. Was the pressure monitored while pushing the cuticles to avoid damaging the cuticles and nail plate?	☐	☐

massage manipulation

	YES	NO
25. Was the massage cream applied to the hand/arm in a sanitary manner?	☐	☐
26. Was the massage cream warmed in the hands first before being applied to the model?	☐	☐
27. Were there smooth, rhythmic massage manipulations?	☐	☐
28. Was there a break in contact with the model's hands or arm during the manipulations?	☐	☐
29. Was the massage cream completely removed from the nails after completing the massage movements?	☐	☐

polish

	YES	NO
30. Was a base coat used and applied properly?	☐	☐
31. Was the polish applied properly?	☐	☐
32. Was a topcoat used and applied properly?	☐	☐
33. Did the polish adequately cover the entire nail?	☐	☐
34. Was the finished polish application smooth and even?	☐	☐
35. Was all of the cuticle and skin area free from polish?	☐	☐

overall

	YES	NO
36. Were all bottles/jars properly capped when not in use?	☐	☐
37. Were all implements and supplies disposed of properly?	☐	☐
38. Were all safety requirements observed?	☐	☐
39. Did the service flow smoothly without interruption?	☐	☐
40. Was the procedure completed within the allotted time frame?	☐	☐

All yes answers are worth 2.5 points. What is the score out of 100?

chapter 13: manicuring review

Complete the multiple-choice questions below by circling the correct answer to each question.

1. What is the most popular nail shape for men?
   a. Round
   b. Square
   c. Pointed
   d. Oval

2. Abrasive boards and buffers typically have one, two, or three different grit surfaces, depending on what?
   a. Type
   b. Use
   c. Style
   d. All of the above

3. Why would you not want to store abrasives or other implements in a plastic bag or other sealed, airtight containers?
   a. It's not sanitary
   b. It's the perfect environment for pathogens to grow and multiply
   c. They could collect moisture and rust or ruin
   d. All of the above

4. What is the purpose of base coat?
   a. Creates a thicker layer of film at the base for added strength
   b. Improves adhesion of polish
   c. Prevents polish from staining the nail
   d. B and C

5. Why is it important to wash your hands before all nail services?
   a. So they are clean and fresh
   b. To prevent the spread of communicable disease
   c. To remove dirt and debris
   d. A and C

6. What can be used in the beginning of a manicure to soften the skin and cuticles?
   a. Water
   b. Lotion and heated mitts
   c. Hand sanitizer
   d. A and B

7. Which of these steps are parts of the client consultation?
   a. Check the nails and skin to make sure that they are healthy
   b. Check that the service you are providing is appropriate
   c. Discuss what the client's expectations are
   d. All of the above

8. What is the advantage to having a paraffin wax hand treatment before a manicure?

    a. It allows the client to have her nails polished immediately at the end of the manicure service.

    b. It enhances rough or callused skin.

    c. It keeps the polish on longer.

    d. All of the above

9. A generic term for any solvent-based, colored film applied to the nail plate for cosmetic purposes is:

    a. UV gel

    b. Overlay

    c. Nail polish

    d. All of the above

10. What might you change for a men's manicure compared to a women's?

    a. Longer, more firm massage

    b. Buffed nails instead of polish

    c. Music and aromatherapy

    d. A and B

11. Abrasives that cannot survive the cleaning and disinfection process without being damaged are considered _____ and must be discarded after a single use.

    a. Re-usable

    b. Disposable

    c. Multi-use

    d. A and C

12. What other marketing terms are used to name the colored film known as nail polish?

    a. Enamel

    b. Lacquer

    c. Varnish

    d. All of the above

13. What evaporates in nail polish to create the solid film that is left on the nail plate?

    a. Nitrocellulose

    b. Solvents

    c. Alcohol

    d. Moisture

14. What determines the drying time of polish?

    a. Amount and type of solvent

    b. Temperature of the salon

    c. Temperature of the client's hands

    d. All of the above

15. Which products are highly flammable?

    a. Nail polish

    b. Base coat

    c. Cuticle oil

    d. A and B

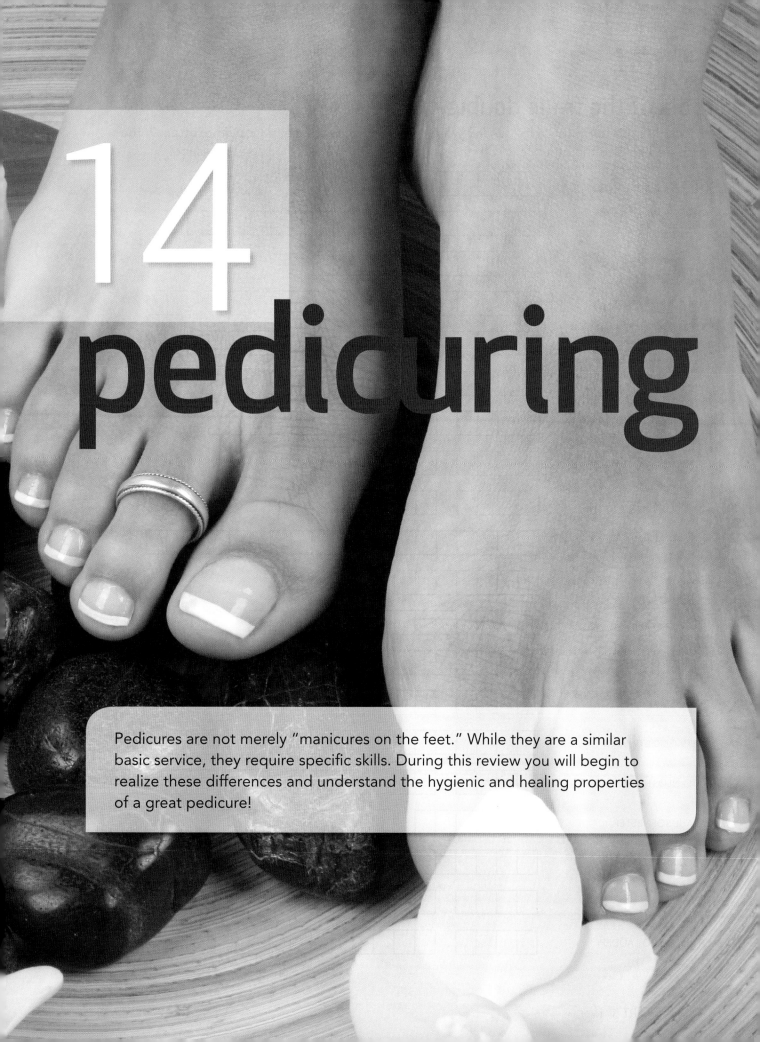

14
pedicuring

Pedicures are not merely "manicures on the feet." While they are a similar basic service, they require specific skills. During this review you will begin to realize these differences and understand the hygienic and healing properties of a great pedicure!

tools of the trade double puzzle!

Unscramble the terms listed below and write the word inside the cells. Copy the letters in the numbered cells to the other cells with the same number to reveal the secret message!

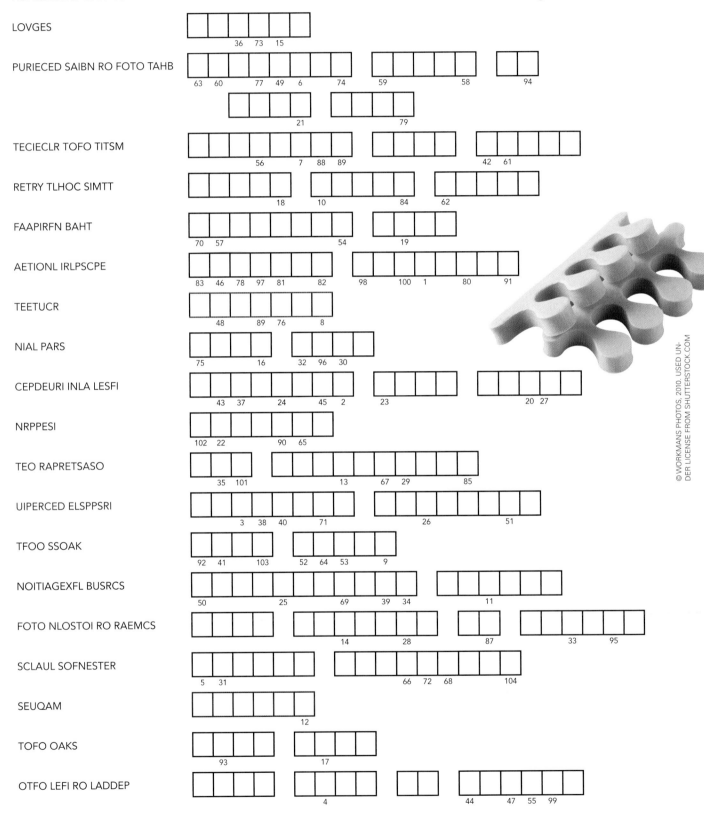

LOVGES

☐☐☐☐☐☐
　36 73 15

PURIECED SAIBN RO FOTO TAHB

☐☐☐☐☐☐☐☐☐　☐☐☐☐☐☐　☐☐
63 60　 77 49 6　 74　 59　　 58　　 94

☐☐☐☐☐　☐☐☐☐☐
　　21　　　 79

TECIECLR TOFO TITSM

☐☐☐☐☐☐☐☐　☐☐☐☐　☐☐☐☐☐
　　56　 7 88 89　　　　　　 42 61

RETRY TLHOC SIMTT

☐☐☐☐☐☐　☐☐☐☐☐☐☐　☐☐☐☐☐
　　18　　 10　　　 84　 62

FAAPIRFN BAHT

☐☐☐☐☐☐☐☐☐☐☐
70 57　　　 54　　 19

AETIONL IRLPSCPE

☐☐☐☐☐☐☐☐☐　☐☐☐☐☐☐☐☐
83 46 78 97 81　 82　 98 100 1　 80　 91

TEETUCR

☐☐☐☐☐☐☐
　48　 89 76　 8

NIAL PARS

☐☐☐☐☐☐　☐☐☐☐☐
75　　 16　 32 96 30

CEPDEURI INLA LESFI

☐☐☐☐☐☐☐☐☐　☐☐☐☐☐　☐☐☐☐☐
43 37　 24　 45 2　 23　　　　　 20 27

NRPPESI

☐☐☐☐☐☐
102 22　　 90 65

TEO RAPRETSASO

☐☐☐☐　☐☐☐☐☐☐☐☐☐☐
35 101　　　 13　 67 29　　 85

UIPERCED ELSPPSRI

☐☐☐☐☐☐☐☐　☐☐☐☐☐☐☐☐☐
　 3 38 40　 71　　 26　　 51

TFOO SSOAK

☐☐☐☐☐☐　☐☐☐☐☐☐
92 41　 103　 52 64 53　 9

NOITIAGEXFL BUSRCS

☐☐☐☐☐☐☐☐☐☐☐　☐☐☐☐☐☐☐
50　　 25　　 69 39 34　　 11

FOTO NLOSTOI RO RAEMCS

☐☐☐☐☐　☐☐☐☐☐☐☐☐☐　☐☐☐☐☐☐
　　　　 14　　 28　　 87　　 33　 95

SCLAUL SOFNESTER

☐☐☐☐☐☐☐　☐☐☐☐☐☐☐☐☐☐☐
 5 31　　　　　　 66 72 68　 104

SEUQAM

☐☐☐☐☐☐
　　 12

TOFO OAKS

☐☐☐☐☐　☐☐☐☐☐
93　　　　 17

OTFO LEFI RO LADDEP

☐☐☐☐☐　☐☐☐☐☐☐　☐☐　☐☐☐☐☐☐☐
　　　 4　　　　　　　 44　 47 55 99

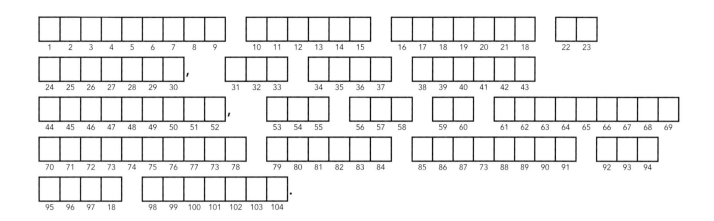

```
[ ][ ][ ][ ][ ][ ][ ][ ][ ]   [ ][ ][ ][ ][ ][ ]   [ ][ ][ ][ ][ ][ ]   [ ][ ]
 1  2  3  4  5  6  7  8  9     10 11 12 13 14 15    16 17 18 19 20 21 18  22 23

[ ][ ][ ][ ][ ][ ][ ] ,   [ ][ ][ ]   [ ][ ][ ][ ]   [ ][ ][ ][ ][ ][ ]
24 25 26 27 28 29 30      31 32 33    34 35 36 37    38 39 40 41 42 43

[ ][ ][ ][ ][ ][ ][ ][ ][ ] ,   [ ][ ][ ]   [ ][ ][ ]   [ ][ ][ ][ ][ ][ ][ ][ ][ ][ ][ ]
44 45 46 47 48 49 50 51 52       53 54 55    56 57 58    59 60 61 62 63 64 65 66 67 68 69

[ ][ ][ ][ ][ ][ ][ ][ ][ ][ ]   [ ][ ][ ][ ][ ][ ]   [ ][ ][ ][ ][ ][ ][ ]   [ ][ ][ ]
70 71 72 73 74 75 76 77 73 78    79 80 81 82 83 84    85 86 87 73 88 89 90 91  92 93 94

[ ][ ][ ][ ]   [ ][ ][ ][ ][ ][ ][ ] .
95 96 97 18    98 99 100 101 102 103 104
```

Fun Fact...

A quarter of all the bones in the human body are down in your feet.

Source: http://www.podiatrychannel.com/anatomy/index.shtml

Pedicure Pre-Service

mini quiz: pedicure pre-service

List the steps in the pedicure pre-service procedure.

Cleaning and Disinfecting

1. _____

_____

_____

_____

_____

2. _____

_____

_____

_____

_____

3. _____

_____

_____

_____

_____

_____

4. _____

_____

_____

_____

_____

_____

_____

_____

_____

5. _____

_____

_____

_____

_____

Table Set-Up

6. _____

_____

_____

_____

_____

_____

7. _____

_____

_____

_____

_____

_____

8. _____

_____

_____

_____

_____

_____

_____

9. _____

_____

_____

_____

_____

_____

_____

10. _____

_____

_____

_____

_____

11. _____

_____

_____

_____

_____

12. _____

_____

_____

_____

_____

13. _____

_____

_____

_____

_____

Greet Client

14. _____

_____

_____

_____

15. _____

_____

_____

_____

16. _____

_____

_____

_____

_____

_____

Pedicure Service

unscramble these basic pedicure steps

Put these basic pedicure steps in order by writing in the number 1-11. Then describe what's happening in each photo on the lines provided.

Step _____

_____

_____

_____

Step _____

_____

_____

_____

Step _____

_____

_____

_____

State Board Exam NOTES

It is illegal for nail technicians to cut or dramatically reduce calluses on clients unless working under the direct supervision of a physician or podiatrist. Cutting falls under the category of medical treatment, and is not a cosmetic service.

Step _____

_____

_____

_____

Step _____

_____

_____

_____

Step _____

_____

_____

_____

Step _____

_____

_____

_____

Step _____

_____

_____

_____

Step _____

_____

_____

_____

Step _____

_____

_____

_____

_____

massage practice

Find a partner to practice the foot and leg massage from Procedure 14-4 of your textbook. Set up your "client" at a pedicure station and have them score you 1-10 on the steps below.

Tech Tip:

Make copies of this exercise so you can continue to get feedback when you practice your foot and leg massage.

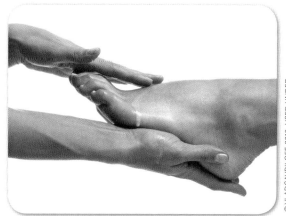

massage evaluation

1 = unorganized, painful, uncomfortable or skipped all together.

10 = organized, relaxing and enjoyable experience.

☐ 1. **Apply Lotion.** Gently apply lotion or oil to foot and leg being massaged.

☐ 2. **Ankle Rotations.** Rotate the entire foot in a circular motion.

☐ 3. **Palm slides.** Place the base of your palm on top of foot behind the toes and slide up to the ankle area with gentle pressure. Repeat 3 to 5 times in the middle, then on the sides of the dorsal side of the foot. Ever so slightly lift the palm each time to return to the initial position after reaching the ankle.

☐ 4. **Plantar Relaxation.** Place the thumb on the plantar surface of the foot with the fingers gently holding the dorsal side of the foot. Now, slide the other hand to same position on the foot, opposite side. Move one thumb in a firm, circular movement, moving from one side of the foot, across, above the heel, up the medial side (center side) of the foot to below the toes, across the ball of the foot and back down the other side of the foot (distal side) to the original position; now, move the thumb of the other hand across and up the outside of the foot, then down to its original position. Repeat 3 to 5 times.

☐ **5. Heel Relaxation.** Perform the same thumb movement on the surface of the heels, rotating your thumbs in opposite directions. Repeat 3 to 5 times.

☐ **6. Instep Friction.** Place your one hand on top of the foot, cupping it, and make a fist with your other hand. The hand on top of the foot will press the foot towards you while your other hand twists into the instep of the foot. Repeat 3 to 5 times.

☐ **7. Toe massage.** Start with the little toe, using the thumb on top and index finger on bottom of the toe. Hold each toe and rotate the thumb in a circle. Start at base of toe and work toward the end of the toes, gently squeezing the tip of each toe once; then move to the next toe. Repeat 3 to 5 times on each toe.

☐ **8. Toe Rotation.** Hold the tip of the toe, starting with the little toe, and make a figure eight with each toe. Repeat 3 to 5 times.

☐ **9. Front Leg Slides.** Grasp (gently) the client's leg from behind the ankle with one hand. On the front of the leg with the other hand, perform effleurage movements from the ankle to below the knee. Move up the leg and then lightly return to the original location. Perform 5 to 7 repetitions, then move to the sides of the leg and perform 5 to 7 repetitions.

☐ **10. Back Leg Slides.** Slide to the back of the leg and perform effleurage movements up the back of the leg. Stroke up the leg, then, with less pressure, return to the original location; perform 5 to 7 times.

☐ **11. Wrap and Repeat.** Wrap the massaged foot in a dry terrycloth towel and move to the other foot. Repeat all steps on the other foot and leg.

☐ **12. Ending.** Place both of the client's feet on the foot rest. Press your entire hands 3 times onto the feet. (Not a hard press, just a firm push.) Maintain each press for 1-2 seconds. After the last press, lift your palms slightly, but maintain contact with the feet with your finger tips. Now, gently pull you hand toward the tips of the toes with a feather-light touch of your fingertips. Pull completely off the end of the toes.

☐ **13.** Were the motions fluid and relaxing?

☐ **14.** Did it feel like the technician knew what she/he was doing?

☐ **15.** Did the technician keep one hand in contact with the client at all times, even if lotion needed to be reapplied?

☐ **16.** Rate the entire experience overall.

Tech **Tip:**

Review the score sheet and recognize where you need to improve. Keep these sheets as a reference to track your progress as you continue to practice.

Fun **Fact...**

The foot contains 26 bones, 33 joints, 107 ligaments and 19 muscles.

Source: http://www.orthospecmd.com/TheFootandAnkle.html

chapter 14: pedicuring review

Complete the multiple-choice questions below by circling the correct answer to each question.

1. Callus softener products are applied directly to the _____ and left on for a short period of time, according to the manufacturers' directions, to soften and smooth thickened tissue.
   a. Heels
   b. Bottom of the foot
   c. Over pressure points
   d. A and C

2. What materials are specially designed for use in pedicures?
   a. Toe separators
   b. Pedicure slippers
   c. Gloves
   d. A and B

3. What additional procedure is included in a spa pedicure in most salons that is not included in a basic pedicure?
   a. Foot massage
   b. Leg massage
   c. Polish
   d. Callus remover

4. What method of therapeutic manipulation of the body includes rubbing, pinching, kneading, and tapping?
   a. Reflexology
   b. Reiki
   c. Massage
   d. None of the above

5. Foot paddles are designed to:
   a. Remove calluses
   b. Smooth and reduce dry, flaky skin
   c. Smooth foot calluses
   d. B and C

6. A pedicure is a cosmetic service performed on the feet by a licensed nail technician that includes:
   a. Trimming and shaping the nails
   b. Exfoliating the skin
   c. A foot massage
   d. All of the above

7. What is the method called that includes applying pressure with thumb and fingers to the hands and feet to promote demonstrated health benefits?
   a. Reflexology
   b. Reiki
   c. Shiatsu massage
   d. All of the above

8. The accepted time between pedicure appointments is:
   a. Two weeks
   b. Three weeks
   c. Four weeks
   d. Six weeks

9. How many minutes should you circulate the EPA-registered hospital disinfectant through the whirlpool spa or air-jet basin when disinfecting after every client?
   a. 5 minutes
   b. 10 minutes
   c. 15 minutes
   d. 20 minutes

10. Some improvements in the feet require more than one appointment and are referred to as:
    a. Re-booking
    b. A series
    c. Long term improvement
    d. Short term improvement

11. Which of these are add-on services and should include an extra charge?
    a. Paraffin wax treatments
    b. Polish
    c. Nail art
    d. A and C

12. Many salons and spas have found that selling manicure and pedicure packages helps increase business and increases revenue. How would you create or promote this?
    a. With themed services for holidays, such as a Valentine's mani/pedi for two
    b. With seasonal products included, such as pumpkin spice mani/pedi with pumpkin scented lotions and scrubs
    c. With unique results, such as anti-aging mani/pedi or skin rejuvenation mani/pedi
    d. All of the above

13. Why are elderly clients perfect candidates for a pedicure?
    a. Some cannot reach their feet.
    b. They enjoy visiting the salon weekly.
    c. Some cannot see their toes well.
    d. A and C

14. Why should the foot be grasped between the thumb and fingers at the mid-tarsal area when performing a pedicure, with the thumb on the bottom of the foot, while the fingers are wrapped around the dorsal side of the foot?

    a. It's a comfortable position for the nail technician.

    b. To lock the foot into place, allowing the nail technician control of its movements.

    c. To increase circulation in the clients foot.

    d. A and B

15. To keep your whirlpool foot spa disinfected correctly, you should do this at the end of everyday.

    a. Clean screen and removable parts with a brush and liquid soap and water.

    b. Circulate chelating detergent through the system for 5-10 minutes.

    c. Circulate EPA-registered hospital disinfectant through the basin for ten minutes.

    d. All of the above

what would you do? a salon **scenario**

It's a Saturday afternoon in June, prime pedicure season, and you have 5 pedicures booked 45 minutes apart. How will you manage to properly disinfect your whirlpool foot spa between each client?

_____

_____

_____

_____

_____

_____

_____

_____

_____

_____

_____

15 electric filing

Electric files are very safe when used by trained nail technicians and can provide many benefits besides speeding up the time spent on a service. So let's review what to look for when purchasing your electric file and bits, how the electric file is used and some important safety tips associated with electric filing.

electric filing double puzzle

Unscramble the electric filing terms listed below and write the word inside the cells. Copy the letters in the numbered cells to the other cells with the same number to reveal the secret message!

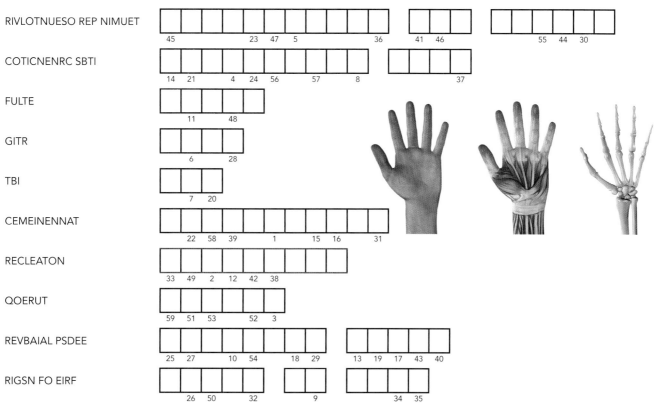

RIVLOTNUESO REP NIMUET

45   23 47 5   36   41 46   55 44 30

COTICNENRC SBTI

14 21   4 24 56   57   8   37

FULTE

11   48

GITR

6   28

TBI

7   20

CEMEINENNAT

22 58 39   1   15 16   31

RECLEATON

33 49 2 12 42 38

QOERUT

59 51 53   52 3

REVBAIAL PSDEE

25 27   10 54   18 29   13 19 17 43 40

RIGSN FO EIRF

26 50   32   9   34 35

Clues

1. RPM; number of times a bit turns in a complete circle in one minute.
2. Balanced bits that do not wobble or vibrate.
3. Long, slender, cut or groove found on carbide bits.
4. Number of abrasive particles per square inch.
5. Filing tool that inserts into the handpiece that actually does the filing.
6. When a nail enhancement needs to be serviced after two or more weeks from the initial application of the nail enhancement product.
7. The tightness of the inside of the shank where the bit fits into the handpiece.
8. Power of machine or its ability to keep turning when applying pressure during filing.
9. A complete range of speed from lowest to highest instead of just the traditional high, medium, low speed options.
10. Grooves carved into the nail caused by filing with bits at the incorrect angle.

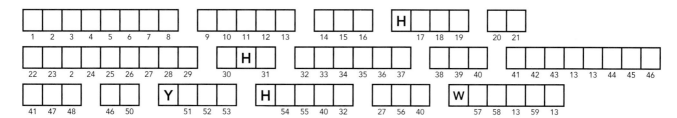

Choosing An Electric File And Bits

buying an electric nail file

List eight features you should look for in an electric nail file.

1. _____

2. _____

3. _____

4. _____

5. _____

6. _____

7. _____

8. _____

Fun **Fact...**

Electric files that are purchased at craft, hobby and tool stores have a tremendous amount of vibration that can damage the natural nail; microshatter monomer and polymer nail enhancements; and cause wrist damage to the nail tech.

identify these bits

Identify the following electric file bits by writing the name of the bit under the photo.

1. _____ 2. _____

COURTESY OF MEDICOOL, INC.

3. _____

© MILADY, A PART OF CENGAGE LEARNING.
PHOTOGRAPHY BY DINO PETROCELLI.

4. _____

COURTESY OF MEDICOOL, INC.

5. _____

COURTESY OF ATWOOD INDUSTRIES.

6. _____

COURTESY OF MEDICOOL, INC.

7. _____

© MILADY, A PART OF CENGAGE LEARNING.
PHOTOGRAPHY BY DINO PETROCELLI.

8. _____

COURTESY OF ATWOOD INDUSTRIES.

9. _____

COURTESY OF ATWOOD INDUSTRIES.

10. _____

© MILADY, A PART OF CENGAGE LEARNING.
PHOTOGRAPHY BY DINO PETROCELLI.

COURTESY OF MEDICOOL, INC.

11. _____

12. _____

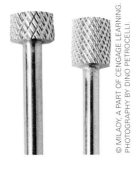

© MILADY, A PART OF CENGAGE LEARNING.
PHOTOGRAPHY BY DINO PETROCELLI.

COURTESY OF MEDICOOL, INC.

13. _____

14. _____

COURTESY OF MEDICOOL, INC.

© MILADY, A PART OF CENGAGE LEARNING.
PHOTOGRAPHY BY TREVOR EHMANN.

15. _____

16. _____

COURTESY OF MEDICOOL, INC.

17. _____

electric file mini quiz

Answer the questions about using an electric file in the space provided.

1. What two things can you use to dramatically enhance the shine of nails?

   _____

2. Explain the difference between the particles that these three different bits make and what happens to those particles when using an electric file.

   Diamond bits: _____

   Carbide bits: _____

   _____

   Sanders or Sleeves: _____

   _____

3. How do you measure grit?

   _____

4. How are carbide bits measured?

   _____

5. Name and explain two basic kinds of carbide bits.

   a. _____

   b. _____

   _____

6. What are diamond bits?

   _____

   _____

7. If the edges of a bit are sharp, what should you do?

   _____

8. List the three ways to clean a bit before disinfecting.

a. _____

b. _____

c. _____

9. How do you disinfect bits?

a. _____

b. _____

c. _____

d. _____

10. What can happen if you drop your bit while in the handpiece?

_____

Safety For Electric Filing

safety facts

It is important that you understand and remember the basic safety tips for electric filing. Circle true or false about the following safety tips for using an electric file mentioned below.

T   F   **1.** Keep your long hair tied back or put it up so that that it is not caught in the handpiece.

T   F   **2.** Never angle the client's hand when using the handpiece.

T   F   **3.** Compensate for speed with pressure. If you feel that you need to press harder, then reduce speed and apply more pressure to the nail.

T   F   **4.** Keep the bit parallel to the nail.

T   F   **5.** Wear a dust mask during filing to avoid inhaling dust particles.

T   F   **6.** Receive the proper education before using any machine or product.

T   F   **7.** Wear eye protection when filing to avoid dust particles from getting into the eyes.

T   F   **8.** Never lift the bit when filing.

T   F   **9.** Do not use bits in a heavy-handed or aggressive way.

T   F   **10.** Keep the bit at a 45-degree angle when shortening the free edge to avoid skipping.

chapter 15: electric filing review

Complete the multiple-choice questions below by circling the correct answer to each question.

1. What should a maintenance service accomplish?
   a. Artificial extension of the natural nail
   b. Application of enhancement product on the new growth of nail
   c. Rebalance the nail to ensure its strength, shape and durability
   d. B and C

2. Because the motor is in the hand piece, all professional electric files are called
   a. Nail professional electric files
   b. Micromotor machines
   c. Anti-vibration machines
   d. None of the above

3. RPM capacity of electric files can vary from 0 to
   a. 5,000
   b. 15,000
   c. 25,000
   d. 35,000

4. Bits that are balanced while spinning are called:
   a. Concentric
   b. Balancing bits
   c. Barrel bits
   d. Level

5. What type of bit shaves the surface of the nail as it files?
   a. Sleeves
   b. Sanders
   c. Carbide
   d. Diamond

6. What type of bits can safely file the cuticle area and sides of the nail because of their rounded ends?
   a. Diamond
   b. Natural nail discs
   c. Carbides
   d. Swiss carbides

7. You know your drill speed is too slow when it:
   a. Creates rings of fire
   b. Starts grabbing
   c. Bogs down
   d. All of the above

8. The use of _____ can reduce heat and hold dust to the surface of the bit.
    a. Buffing cream
    b. Buffing oil
    c. Water
    d. B and C

9. Skipping occurs when the bit looses contact with the nail and skips or jumps across the nail because:
    a. The speed is too high
    b. The speed is too low
    c. There is a lack of control of the file
    d. There's too much vibration

10. What can cause pain, swelling or injury to the wrist, elbow, shoulder arms, or back?
    a. Poor posture
    b. Repetitive motions
    c. Lack of sleep
    d. All of the above

11. High vibration is something to avoid when using an electric file. Vibration can:
    a. Create microshattering with enhancement products
    b. Cause bits shanks to bend
    c. Be harmful to the nail professional's hand, wrist, and arm
    d. A and C

12. Buffing bits can be made from:
    a. Leather
    b. Goat's hair
    c. Cotton rag
    d. All of the above

13. What bit should you use to shorten the nail?
    a. Barrel bit
    b. Cone bit
    c. UNC bit
    d. Football bit

14. Which of these four bits would you use to repair a crack?
    a. Flat-tipped barrel bit
    b. UNC bit
    c. Cone bit
    d. Needle bit

Diane finally comes in for maintenance after four weeks of wearing her pink and white monomer liquid and polymer powder nail enhancements using forms. She has broken two nails off at the stress area, two nails are cracked on the side, and all eight remaining have new growth at the cuticle area and at the smile line. Using your electric file for this maintenance, what will you do to repair Diane's nails back to perfection?

_____

_____

_____

_____

_____

_____

_____

_____

_____

_____

_____

_____

_____

_____

_____

16 nail tips and wraps

One of the most popular services that a nail professional can offer clients is the opportunity to wear beautiful nails in an almost endless variety of lengths and strengths.

Regardless of whether a client is interested in wearing long, medium, or short nails, a nail tip can be applied and trimmed to any length. Once the tip is applied, you and your client will have an opportunity to choose from a variety of products that can be layered over the natural nail and the tip to further secure the strength of the nail and its beauty.

We will now begin to review some of those overlay options. In this chapter, we will learn about nail wraps: the fabrics, the looks, the strengths and of course how they are applied. Let's begin!

nail tips and wraps puzzle

Fill in the crossword puzzle with key words found in chapter 16, by using the clues below.

ACROSS

3 Nail wrap made of silk, linen, or fiberglass.

6 Strip of fabric cut to 1/8" in length and applied to the weak point of the nail.

9 A layer of any kind of nail enhancement product that is applied over the natural nail or nail and tip application for added strength.

10 Plastic, pre-molded nails shaped from a tough polymer made from ABS plastic.

12 The bonding agent used to secure the nail tip to the natural nail.

13 Piece of fabric cut to completely cover a crack or break in the nail.

15 Very thin synthetic mesh with a loose weave.

18 The point where the free edge of the natural nail meets the tip.

DOWN

1 A broad category of overlays that use nail wrap resin to affix the overlay to the natural nail and nail tip.
2 A term used when a nail enhancement needs to be serviced.
4 A product specially designed to help adhesives dry quicker.
5 Used to coat and secure fabric wraps.
7 Implement designed especially for use on nail tips.
8 Temporary nail wrap made of very thin paper.
11 A substance used to remove surface moisture and tiny amounts of oil left on the natural nail plate.
14 A common thermoplastic used to make light, rigid, molded nail tips.
16 Closely woven, heavy fabric used for nail wraps.
17 A strong, glossy, tightly woven natural fiber used for nail wrapping that becomes transparent when wrap resin is applied.

Nail Tips and Wraps

tools of the trade double puzzle

Use the clues to help you identify the special products and implements needed for the application and removal of nail tips and wraps. Write your answer inside the cells and then copy the letters in the numbered cells, to the cells with the same number to reveal the secret message!

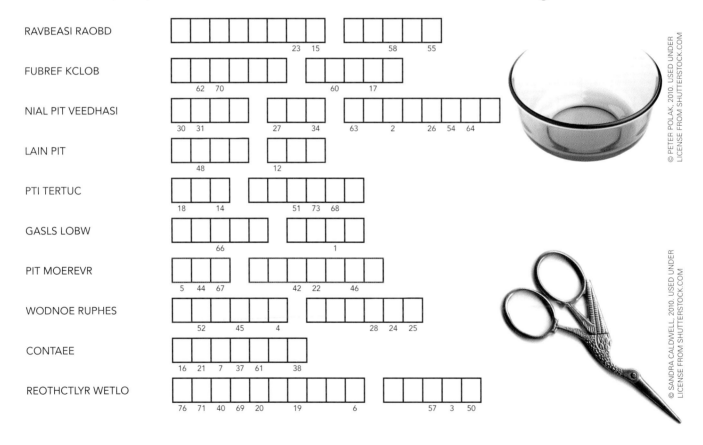

RAVBEASI RAOBD

23 15   58 55

FUBREF KCLOB

62 70   60 17

NIAL PIT VEEDHASI

30 31   27 34   63 2 26 54 64

LAIN PIT

48   12

PTI TERTUC

18 14   51 73 68

GASLS LOBW

66   1

PIT MOEREVR

5 44 67   42 22 46

WODNOE RUPHES

52 45 4   28 24 25

CONTAEE

16 21 7 37 61 38

REOTHCTLYR WETLO

76 71 40 69 20 19   6   57 3 50

CABRIF
74 9   75

WARP RISNE
36   56   8

PAWR REINS CAETARELROC
47   43 10   49   41

LMLAS SOISSRSC
11 35   72 32

MSLLA IECPE FO SCTIPLA
33   13 29 65   39   59 53

Clues

1. Used to shape or smooth the nail, removes surface shine.
2. For smoothing.
3. To secure the nail tip to the natural nail.
4. Assortment for application.
5. Used to trim nail tips to the desired length.
6. Holds the solution when removing tips or wraps.
7. A solution you can soak in to remove product.
8. Used to slide off the nail tip.
9. A solution you can soak in to remove product.
10. Covers the hands and bowl when soaking the nails to avoid evaporation of the solution.
11. Cut to cover the surface of the natural nail and the nail tip, to strengthen the enhancement.
12. Used to coat and secure fabric wraps.
13. The dryer that speeds up the hardening process of the wrap resin.
14. Used to cut fabric.
15. Used to press fabric onto the nail plate and prevents the transfer of oil and debris from your fingers.

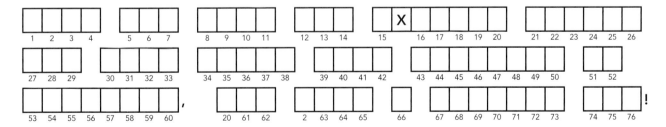

CHAPTER 16 Nail Tips and Wraps   **147**

Fun Fact...

Animal glue, a gelatin made from hides, hooves, or bones, was probably known in prehistoric times as a synthetic adhesive. It remained the leading adhesive until the 20th century.

Source: http://education.yahoo.com/reference/encyclopedia/entry/adhesive

tips and wraps mini quiz

Answer the questions in the space provided about the application, repair, and maintenance of nail tips and wraps.

1. Besides not being aesthetically pleasing, what two things can happen when a nail tip is narrower than the nail plate?

_____

_____

2. If you do not have a tip that provides a perfect fit, what should you do?

_____

_____

3. To save time blending the tip after it is applied, what should you do?

_____

_____

4. Explain the three steps you should use when applying tips.

_____

_____

_____

_____

5. Fabric wraps are made from three different fabrics. What are they? Describe their unique characteristics.

   1. _____

   _____

   2. _____

   _____

   3. _____

   _____

   _____

6. How should you use a plastic sheet as part of a fabric wrap service?

_____

_____

_____

_____

_____

7. What is the protocol for a two-week maintenance visit?

_____

_____

_____

_____

8. What maintenance should be done at the four-week service?

_____

_____

_____

_____

_____

9. How is fabric applied to reinforce a weak point?

_____

_____

_____

10. How is fabric used to repair a break or crack?

_____

_____

_____

_____

nail wrap application puzzle

Complete the steps of the nail wrap application by filling in the missing words. Then find your answers in the word find puzzle on the following page.

Tech Tip:

Some words are used more than once.

1. Perform a complete pre-service _____ and _____ procedure.

2. Do a standard table set-up, and add all _____ and _____ needed to perform a fabric wrap service.

3. Greet client and ask her to _____ her hands with _____ and _____, and dry them thoroughly.

4. Check for nail _____.

5. Remove existing _____.

6. _____ nails.

7. Push back _____ and remove _____ tissue.

8. Remove oily _____.

9. Apply nail _____.

10. Apply nail _____, if desired.

11. Cut _____.

12. Apply fabric _____.

13. Apply _____.

14. Trim _____.

15. Apply _____.

16. Apply _____ _____.

17. Apply _____ coat of _____.

18. Apply _____ coat of wrap resin accelerator.

19. _____ and _____ nails.

20. _____ wrap nail.

21. Remove traces of _____.

22. Apply _____.

```
S U T V U L H Z C D F E Z B O C F J C R
E H G B J U J F E K P L J O U Q F E O G
C K S K A T F H J O E E L T K F X T W V
O K I I Y P Y E N B G W I S F X A S G B
N I E P L D M Y W N J C P F Y R G E L D
D I I D R O C W I W L I U Z E V D I L R
W D N A M H P N R E T B U L D S U L E F
C D T O I E A Z P A R H E A V T I P D O
D O H U I E N A R O P C C L E A N P S I
R U M Q L T O I A S C R W A T E R U H L
B A K C A S C S F A F K E L L H Q S A R
L S N X I Q J E N E W H S S N O X M P A
H C P R W F K I F H R H D L I H B R E E
F S E F A M S V C N I I S T Q N B R O P
H Y A B B E D V B N I D I S O R D E R S
U D R W R I E V Z Z S A D H E S I V E
T I U P M U W A Z V H G I Z B J G S Z J
C W A I M P L E M E N T S D D C F I E Y
C R T C Z S V H L O Y D J L K I C L Z F
W X V P O W L J K Z L O T A J X Q X
```

nail wrap strengths

Place the strength number in front of the wrap material, 1 being the weakest and 4 being the strongest.

_____ silk fabric

_____ linen fabric

_____ fiberglass

_____ paper materials

Fun Fact...

In the 1960's Juliette (paper) nail wraps—the precursor to the now popular silk and fiberglass wraps—were commonly used to protect natural nail tips. Juliettes are credited with establishing the now familiar biweekly nail maintenance appointments. Detached nail tips were reaffixed with model airplane glue and reinforced with thin strands of cotton. Human nail clippings were also used to add nail length. Clients brought their separated nail tips to their nail appointments for reattachment.

nail tip and wrap application mistakes

You've reviewed what products are needed and the procedure steps, but there is still much more to remember for your state board exam. Answer **Yes** or **No** to these questions about common mistakes that can be made during the practical exam.

_____ 1. Should you wash your hands?

_____ 2. Should you have the model wash her hands and nails?

_____ 3. Should there be air bubbles between the natural nail and the nail tip?

_____ 4. Should the nail tip fit from sidewall to sidewall on the model's finger?

_____ 5. Should you file into the natural nail bed when blending the nail tip flush to the natural nail?

_____ 6. Should you hold the abrasive board at an angle when blending the tip to the natural nail?

_____ 7. Should you place the nail tip over the entire nail bed?

_____ 8. Should you properly clean oil, residue, or dust from the nail _before_ applying the nail tip?

_____ 9. When blending the nail tip with the natural nail should you be able to see where the natural nail stops and the tip begins?

_____ 10. Should you wear safety glasses or gloves when using nail adhesive or adhesive?

_____ 11. Should you measure the nail before cutting the fabric?

_____ 12. Should you allow the nail adhesive to adequately dry in between applications?

_____ 13. Should the adhesive touch the cuticle area and the sidewalls of the nails?

_____ 14. Should the nail wrap extend off of the nail's free edge?

_____ 15. Should you clean and disinfect the scissors you use for cutting the wrap fabric?

state board tip and wrap practice exam

Find two students to partner with. Practice your state board tip and wrap application from nail prep to polish on your "student model." During the process have your "student examiner" check yes or no to the questions below.

State Board Tip And Wrap Practical Exam

nail prep

	YES	NO
1. Were the participant's hands cleaned?	☐	☐
2. Were the model's hands cleaned?	☐	☐
3. Was the required cuticle care properly performed?	☐	☐
4. Was the shine removed from the nail adequately and safely?	☐	☐
5. Was dust properly removed from the natural nail?	☐	☐
6. Were oil and any residual products removed completely from the natural nail?	☐	☐
7. Was a nail dehydrator applied to the model's finger before the application of the nail tip was started?	☐	☐

nail tip application

	YES	NO
8. Was the nail tip the adequate size for the model's finger?	☐	☐
9. Was the nail tip properly placed on the model's finger using the stop, rock, and hold method?	☐	☐
10. Were there air bubbles trapped between the tip and natural nail in the well area?	☐	☐
11. Was the nail tip sufficiently blended and flush with the natural nail?	☐	☐
12. Was the abrasive board held flat on the nail while blending to avoid damage or grooves in the nail plate?	☐	☐
13. Was the cuticle area undamaged during filing?	☐	☐
14. Was the sidewall held during filing?	☐	☐
15. Was the uncovered nail plate free from nail adhesive?	☐	☐
16. Was the final shaping of the nail tip adequate?	☐	☐

nail wrap application

	YES	NO
17. Was the fabric cut for the wrap appropriately sized?	☐	☐
18. Was the nail adhesive applied properly to the natural nail?	☐	☐
19. Was the fabric applied smoothly and correctly over the nail plate?	☐	☐
20. Was the resin applied properly over the nail wrap fabric?	☐	☐
21. Was the fabric at least 1.16 inch away from the cuticle area?	☐	☐
22. Were the cuticle and sidewalls of the nail free from the nail adhesive?	☐	☐
23. Was the nail properly filed so as not to disturb the nail wrap fabric?	☐	☐
24. Were the cuticle area and sidewall of the finger free from damage while filing?	☐	☐
25. Was the natural nail adequately covered with product?	☐	☐
26. Did the wrap completely adhere to the entire nail area?	☐	☐
27. Was the completed nail smooth, even, and beveled?	☐	☐

overall

	YES	NO
28. Were all bottles/jars properly capped when not in use?	☐	☐
29. Were all implements and supplies disposed of properly?	☐	☐
30. Were all safety requirements observed?	☐	☐
31. Did the service flow smoothly without interruption?	☐	☐
32. Was the procedure completed within the allotted time frame?	☐	☐

All yes answers are worth 3.125 points. What is the score out of 100? ☐

chapter 16: nail tips and wraps review

Complete the multiple-choice questions below by circling the correct answer to each question.

1. What are nail tips used for?
   a. To add length to the nail
   b. To support a nail enhancement
   c. To strengthen the natural nail
   d. A and B

2. Without an overlay, a nail tip will:
   a. Last 2 weeks
   b. Only last a week
   c. Break easily
   d. Crack at the corners

3. When applying a tip that has a well, be sure that _____ when adhering it to the nail.
   a. The well butts up to the natural nail
   b. There are no air bubbles in the adhesive
   c. The tip is clear
   d. A and B

4. To ensure a perfect fit and shape for every client, nail tips are available in many:
   a. Sizes
   b. Shapes
   c. Colors
   d. All of the above

5. The _____ is a depression that serves as the point of contact with the nail plate.
   a. Edge
   b. Lip
   c. Well
   d. Crease

6. When a client has nail tips and/or nail wraps, what type of polish remover should you use?
   a. Non-acetone
   b. Acetone based
   c. Oil based
   d. Any of the above

7. Use a _____ abrasive to lightly buff the nail plate and remove shine before applying tips or wraps.
   a. 150 grit zebra
   b. 100 grit white
   c. 180 grit or higher
   d. None of the above

8. What is a nail wrap used for?
   a. To repair natural nails
   b. To cover the nail to hide imperfections
   c. To strengthen natural nails
   d. A and C

9. Where do you apply nail adhesive when affixing fabric to the nail?
   a. On the fabric
   b. On the nail tip
   c. To the center of the nail
   d. A and C

10. You should always leave a _____ margin between the fabric and the sidewalls and eponychium.
   a. 1/4"
   b. 1/8"
   c. 1/16"
   d. 1/32"

11. What can occur when you do not keep adhesive off the skin?
   a. Skin irritation
   b. Infections
   c. Possible lifting/separation
   d. A and C

12. How do you remove traces of oil on an overlay prior to polishing the nails?
   a. Clean the surface of the nail with acetone
   b. Clean the surface of the nail with alcohol
   c. Clean the surface of the nail with non-acetone polish remover
   d. All of the above

13. How often should you maintain fabric wraps?
   a. Once a week
   b. Every two weeks
   c. Every three weeks
   d. At the client's request

14. Dip powder and adhesive enhancements use a fine polymer powder _____ onto the nail, over a completed fabric wrap.
   a. Sprinkled
   b. Brushed
   c. Spooned
   d. A and C

15. Why would you use fabric to create a stress strip?
   a. To strengthen a weak point
   b. To repair a break
   c. To cover the entire surface of the nail
   d. A and B

Emma is one of your favorite clients. She has been in every week for a manicure for almost a year. She loves to maintain her long natural nails and hates it when she gets one little chip in her red polish. Emma arrived today and told you she will be going on a two-week cruise with her husband to Hawaii at the end of the month. She is worried about her nails and how to maintain them while she's gone. What can you suggest to help her maintain her perfect manicure for the two-week trip?

_____

_____

_____

_____

_____

_____

_____

_____

_____

_____

_____

17 monomer liquid and polymer powder

NAIL ENHANCEMENTS

Nail enhancements based on mixing together liquids and powders are commonly referred to as *acrylic* nails. The term *acrylic* actually refers to an entire family of thousands of different substances, but all share important, closely related features. The ingredients in two-part monomer liquid and polymer powder enhancement systems belong to a branch of the acrylic family called *methacrylates*.

In this chapter we will review the chemistry that explains how these products are formed, how they are applied, and how to remain safe when using them.

Key Terms

monomer liquid and polymer powder chemistry

Explain monomer liquid and polymer powder nail enhancement chemistry and how it works by filling in the answers to the crossword below.

ACROSS

1 One unit called a molecule.
3 Process that joins together monomers to create very long polymer chains; also called "polymerization reaction."
7 Forms on the end of the brush, quickly begins to harden.
8 Units.
10 Substance that starts the chain reaction that leads to the creation of very long polymer chains.
12 The initiator that is added to the polymer powder.
13 Many.

DOWN

2 Chemical liquid mixed with polymer powder to form the sculptured nail enhancement.
3 Make products work and behave differently.
4 Substance that speeds up chemical reactions between monomer liquid and polymer powder.
5 Chemical reaction that creates polymers; also called curing or hardening.
6 Powder in white, clear, pink, and many other colors, which is combined with monomer liquid to form the nail enhancement.
9 Substance formed by combining many small molecules (monomers) into very long chain-like structures.
11 One.

Nail Enhancement Structure

label this!

Write the term in the spaces provided on the drawing to describe the structure of the nail enhancement.

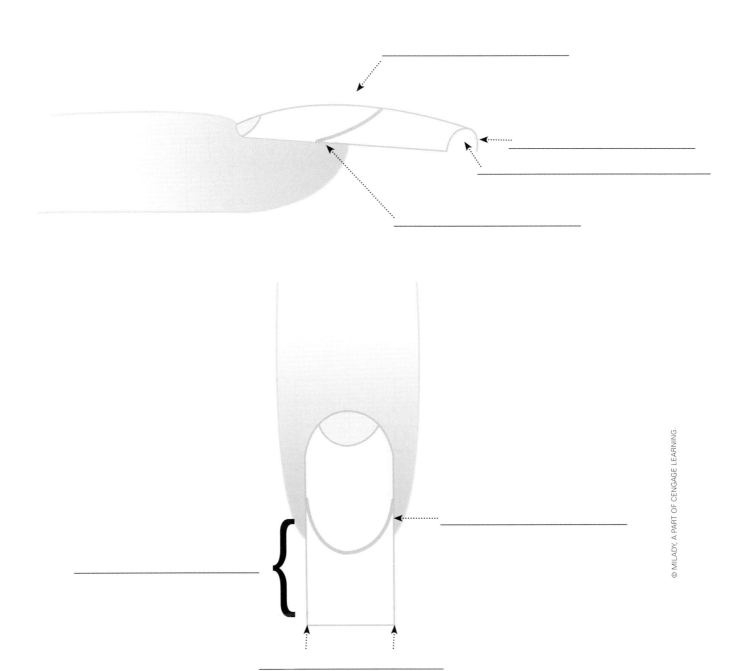

Fun Fact...

Monomer liquid and polymer powder nail services were first offered by nail technicians in the 1970's. Plastic nail tips were also introduced during this time, replacing human nail clippings previously used to add length.

Monomer Liquid And Polymer Powder

tools of the trade double puzzle

Use the clues below to help you identify the products and implements needed for the application and removal of nail tips and wraps. Write your answer inside the cells, and then copy the letters in the numbered cells to the cells with the same number to reveal the secret message!

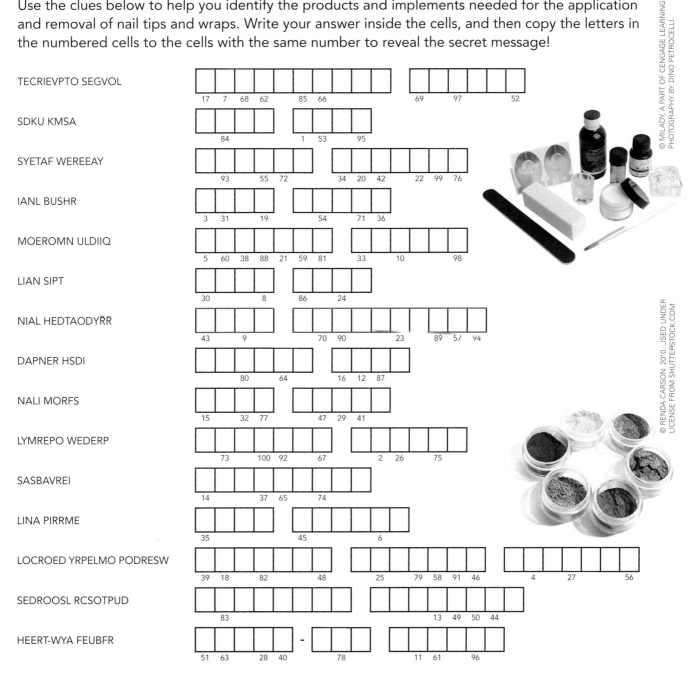

TECRIEVPTO SEGVOL
17 7 68 62 85 66 / 69 97 52

SDKU KMSA
84 / 1 53 95

SYETAF WEREEAY
93 55 72 / 34 20 42 22 99 76

IANL BUSHR
3 31 19 / 54 71 36

MOEROMN ULDIIQ
5 60 38 88 21 59 81 / 33 10 98

LIAN SIPT
30 / 8 86 24

NIAL HEDTAODYRR
43 9 / 70 90 23 / 89 57 94

DAPNER HSDI
80 64 / 16 12 87

NALI MORFS
15 32 77 / 47 29 41

LYMREPO WEDERP
73 100 92 67 / 2 26 75

SASBAVREI
14 37 65 74

LINA PIRRME
35 / 45 6

LOCROED YRPELMO PODRESW
39 18 82 48 / 25 79 58 91 46 / 4 27 56

SEDROOSL RCSOTPUD
83 / 13 49 50 44

HEERT-WYA FEUBFR
51 63 28 40 - 78 / 11 61 96

Clues

1. Used to protect hands.
2. Designed to be worn over the nose and mouth to prevent inhalation of excessive amounts of dust.
3. Protects eyes from flying objects or accidental splashes.
4. Brush for monomer liquid and polymer powder application.
5. Half of a product used to create nail enhancements.
6. Pre-formed extensions.
7. Removes surface moisture and tiny amounts of oil left on the natural nail plate.

8. Special holder for monomer liquid and polymer powder.
9. Used when sculpting an extension to the natural nail.
10. Half of a product used to create nail enhancements.
11. Used to shape and refine the natural nail and enhancements.
12. Used to help enhancements adhere to the natural nail.
13. Used for creating nail art and custom blended shades.
14. Products that contain little to no odor.
15. Used to create a high shine on the enhancement.

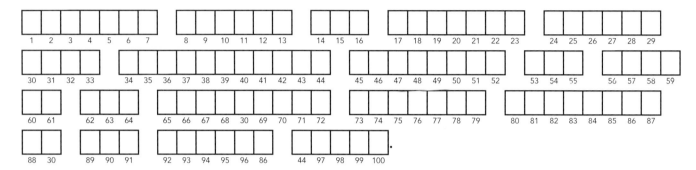

Monomer Liquid And Polymer Powder Application

the one color method puzzle

Fill in the blanks for the procedure to apply one-color monomer liquid and polymer powder nail enhancements over nail tips or natural nails. Then find your answers in the word find puzzle on page 164.

Tech Tip:

Some words are used more than once.

1. _____ nails; remove existing polish.

2. Gently push back _____; carefully remove cuticle.

3. Remove oily _____ from natural nail.

4. Remove nail dust with a clean nylon _____ brush.

5. Apply nail _____.

6. Apply _____ if longer nails are desired.

7. Apply _____.

© MILADY, A PART OF CENGAGE LEARNING. PHOTOGRAPHY BY DINO PETROCELLI.

© MILADY, A PART OF CENGAGE LEARNING. PHOTOGRAPHY BY DINO PETROCELLI.

8. Prepare _____ and
   _____.

9. Dip _____ in monomer liquid.

10. Form a product _____.

11. Place bead in the _____ of the
    _____ of the tip or natural nail.

12. Press and smooth the product to form the entire free
    edge _____.

13. Form product _____.

14. Place bead in the _____ of the nail.

15. Press and smooth the product to form the
    _____.

16. Form product _____.

17. Place bead at the _____ of the nail.

18. Press and smooth the product in the cuticle area leaving a
    tiny margin between product and _____.

19. Glide the brush over the nail to _____
    out imperfections.

20. Repeat application on all remaining _____.

21. _____ nail enhancements.

22. _____ nail enhancements.

23. Apply nail _____.

24. Apply hand cream and _____
    hand and arm.

25. _____ nail enhancements with soap
    and water, dry thoroughly.

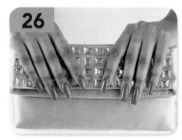

26. Apply nail _____.

```
I Z M J W J N D G L S K A L C K U H J M
H P I I U L D V M W K Q P G N T D C N J
R E D W O P R E M Y L O P P B Z D D E M
G F K T Q T M U I H C Y N O P E Y X A S
B B A S E Z Y W S C S U F N R T S V H
P L A B Y O Q Q G A O F L U O E S K L A
M O N O M E R L I Q U I D T N A U Y N P
R N O L Y H S I L O P K A S G B W T A E
E E A S P I T L I A N R I E F V R U I O
J G T I S K I N C J D O F Y C Q V U L O
K H D N L F Q W H Y N F J Y B P B I S P
G Q G E E P A H H M U V I U D D S I Y H
L U Q U E C R E Y B O R U S E C A Y G P
E E P V C E D I U N Y S N G F U W E R B
L W K L B D R X M S H I N E Z E H Y B P
N B E P A E L F X E B L S B W J B P U L
N A N A I L S L N L R L Z C X R T P F N
N B I G B A B I O Z T L V Y T B H V P J
X E P A L P S O X F E S M O O T H R F B
R L I O V E A G R X C O Q W Y Z O U M V
```

Master Advice On The Two Color Monomer Liquid And Polymer Powder Nail Enhancements Using Forms

This technique, usually referred to by professional nail technicians as French sculpture nails, is one of the most challenging to master. The advice below will assist you while practicing this artistic technique. You may want to have a friend or student read the steps to you as you are working. This will help you remember what to do, and help you to create a pattern, and form good habits. You can also record yourself reading the steps and play it back to yourself as you practice.

French Sculpting Practice Advice from a World Champion Nail Artist!

"In 2005 I won the World Masters Championship in Austria, and $10,000 cash, by creating one set of French Sculpture nails in two and a half hours. This was by no accident! I have been practicing the art of French Sculpture nails since 1996! I learned from a master and now I'm going to pass on some French Sculpting advice to you!

The most difficult part of the two-color monomer liquid and polymer powder nail enhancements is creating the smile line. I've created the steps below to help you practice making that perfect smile line. The example I am showing you is the oval smile line, which is the most beautiful and complementary to the hand. However, smile line shape will vary depending on each client's nail. The most important point when creating a set of French sculpture nails is that all the smile lines are consistent, no matter what the degree or depth. Create a smile line that complements the natural lines of the nail and hand.

It's very important to pay attention to the details, like how you are holding your brush or how you are dipping and wiping your brush on the dappen dish. All these small things will make a huge difference in your application. To perfect this technique it takes many hours of repetition. Get ready to practice!"

— ALISHA RIMANDO

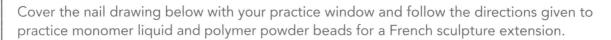

Cover the nail drawing below with your practice window and follow the directions given to practice monomer liquid and polymer powder beads for a French sculpture extension.

1. Dip your brush into the monomer liquid up to the ferrule.

2. Remove brush and gently wipe the side of the brush, half way down the hairs to the tip, against the side of the dappen dish, letting the excess monomer liquid flow out of the tip and back into the dappen dish.

3. Place the brush into the white polymer powder and pick up a medium to large size bead.

MASTER ADVICE: *The bead should have a dry-to-medium, slightly bumpy consistency, not runny or wet, that is large enough to cover the entire free-edge extension up to the edge of the smile line. If it's too wet, wipe it off onto a 4x4 piece of table towel and try again.*

4. Look at the bead and wait for the polymer powder to absorb the monomer liquid, and watch the bead appear smooth, round and shiny. This should take a few seconds.

5. Dab your brush against a 4x4 paper towel to remove any excess liquid still remaining in the brush.

6. Place the bead in the center of the extension edge area of the drawing. There is a circle with an "X" drawn on the first nail to show you where to place the bead. Do not set the bead down at the stress point on the smile line!

MASTER ADVICE: *The bead should settle inside the circle drawing and still be about a 1/4" thick. If it's too big or too small, you should adjust the size of your bead. If it runs outside the lines of the circle after you place it down, the bead was too wet. If the bead doesn't settle and become creamy, it's too dry.*

7. Make at least 10 perfect beads before moving on to step 2.

(Continues)

8. Gently pull your brush across your paper towel, dip into your monomer liquid, then pull your brush across your paper towel again. This will clean your brush.

MASTER ADVICE: *Step 8 will be referred to as "clean your brush" in the directions below. You should do this every minute or two while working with wet product so that product does not get stuck in the hairs.*

step 2 / CREATING THE EXTENSION EDGE

Clean your practice window and follow the directions given to practice monomer liquid and polymer powder French sculpture extension edges.

1. Create the perfect bead.

2. Place it down in the center of the extension edge area of the drawing.

3. Clean your brush.

4. Place the belly of your brush parallel to the table and gently guide the bead to the right corner of the smile line, pressing as you get closer to the corner. The smile line has been drawn in for you as a guide for the first five nails.

MASTER ADVICE: *Pressing the bead near the corners ensures that the product close to the sidewall stays thin, and the thickness stays in the center of the nail or the apex.*

5. Clean your brush.

6. Repeat step 4 for the left corner.

7. Clean your brush.

8. Gently press the belly of the brush in the middle of the bead and stretch the bead toward the edge of the nail drawing. Use the sides of your brush to push the product back inside the picture when it goes over the lines.

MASTER ADVICE: *Notice how you use the brush to shape the nail extension. You will use these same motions to shape the extension edge when following the lines on the nail form.*

9. Clean your brush and make it into a flat edge

10. Use the side edge of the brush to push in the smile line according to the drawing.

11. Smooth over the top surface of the nail.

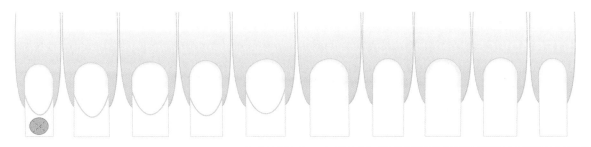

step 3 / ADDING THE CORNERS

Add in the corners of the smile line to create a perfect and more dramatic French look.

1. Pick up a very tiny bead using the same methods for creating the perfect bead.

2. Wipe the tiny bead onto the right corner of the smile line to fill in the tiny triangle left blank.

3. Clean your brush and bring to a point.

4. Wipe the smile line from the center to the right corner to clean the line and extend the product up into the corner.

5. Continue wiping the smile line until the product stops moving.

6. Repeat on left side.

MASTER ADVICE: *The more you practice this, the better you will be. Practice this on all 10 nail drawings at least once before moving on. When you're finished turn the sheet so the practice nails are pointing away from you. How do your smile lines look now?*

step 4 / COMPLETING THE APPLICATION

Now it's time to add the pink polymer powder!

1. Clean your practice window.

2. Create a white extension edge and add in the corners.

3. Dip your brush in the monomer liquid up to the ferrule.

4. Gently wipe the edge of the brush from ferrule to tip, across the dappen dish, to remove excess liquid.

5. Place your brush in the pink powder and pick up a small to medium size bead.

MASTER ADVICE: *Pink beads should appear round, smooth and shiny almost immediately.*

6. Place the bead in the center of the nail plate.

7. Clean your brush, and flatten.

8. Use the flat edge to guide the bead to the cuticle area, pressing it thin as it gets closer. Just before touching the skin, pull the brush toward the extension edge and blend the product toward the white.

MASTER ADVICE: *Keep the brush parallel with the nail when brushing over the surface to ensure you are smoothing the top and not sweeping wet product to another area of the nail.*

9. Clean your brush, and pick up another small to medium size bead of product.

(Continues)

10. Look at the nail from the side and place the bead in the low spot where the apex should be. Wait a second to allow the product to self-level.

11. Clean your brush. Gently pat the product so that it remains in the apex area.

12. Once the stress area is shaped, smooth the top surface of the entire nail.

MASTER ADVICE: *Your application should look very close to the final length, thickness and shape of the finished look. This means that you will have to pay close attention to the size of your beads and ensure that your product doesn't get too thick!*

CHALLENGE: *Can you make the smile lines on the last five nails look like the smile lines on the first five?*

step 5 / PRACTICE ON A LIVE MODEL

The best way to practice sculptured nails is practicing on yourself! You are always available and you always show up on time, and you don't mind if your nails are not perfect in the beginning!

1. Properly prepare your cuticle area and shape the free edge.

2. Buff your nail to a high shine (if you are just practicing and not planning on wearing the nail).

3. Place the form on your nail.

MASTER ADVICE: *Check to ensure the form fits snuggly under the free edge, and above eponychium. Ensure there are no gaps or spaces where product can flow under the form.*

4. Create a perfect bead. If it's not perfect, do not put it on the form. Wipe it off and try again.

5. Create the extension edge. Ensure that you follow the lines on the form that come straight out from your sidewalls.

MASTER ADVICE: *If you make the nail to narrow and it does not reach from sidewall to sidewall, it will have glitches when you finish filing, and will break or crack within a few days of wear.*

6. When you are finished practicing, add in the corners and then add the two pink beads.

MASTER ADVICE: *Removing the product over and over from the form is easy when practicing. Just use a wooden pusher to slide it off the form. Any product that is on the nail will be more difficult to remove and may require soaking in product remover, so do not add the corners and the pink if you are planning to spend some time practicing.*

MASTER ADVICE: *Practice the extension edge on your own nail, every spare moment you have in school and in between clients when you start work in the salon. If you master this first bead, you will be able to master the entire sculpture nail procedure! This is the hardest part.*

Fun Fact...

Don't build your mistake! Many technicians will see a dip here and a dent there and add in small beads of product to fix the mistake. What they are actually doing is building a bigger mistake! Most of the time if there are small dips in the nail, they will disappear when you file. If you continue to add product, you will create a nice smooth surface that is twice as thick as it's supposed to be. Now you've wasted time and product building it, and you will waste more time trying to file it thin! Not to mention, overfilling and lots of vibration on freshly applied product can cause the product to separate from the nail and create lifting problems within the first 48 hours of application.

Maintenance, Repairs And Removal

monomer liquid and polymer powder mini quiz

Answer the questions in the space provided about the repair, maintenance and removal of monomer liquid and polymer powder nail enhancements.

1. What is a nail maintenance?

_____

_____

2. If you are using a pink-and-white product application during a nail maitenance, what color product should you apply first and why?

_____

_____

_____

3. How do you know the nails are completely cured and ready to file?

_____

_____

_____

4. If the nail has a glitch or small chunk taken out of the extension, how will you make this repair?

_____

_____

_____

5. How would you remove a crack?

_____

_____

_____

_____

© MILADY, A PART OF CENGAGE LEARNING. PHOTOGRAPHY BY DINO PETROCELLI.

6. Describe how to safely remove acrylic nail enhancements?

_____

_____

_____

_____

_____

_____

_____

_____

© MILADY, A PART OF CENGAGE LEARNING. PHOTOGRAPHY BY DINO PETROCELLI.

7. After nail enhancements have been removed, why do the nail plates appear to be thinner?

_____

_____

_____

8. How often should clients wearing nail enhancements have a maintenance service, and what does this depend on?

_____

_____

_____

_____

9. Explain why nippers should not be used to loosen nail enhancement product.

_____

_____

_____

10. When using an electric file for the maintenance procedure, explain which bits are needed and what their uses are.

_____

_____

_____

_____

_____

_____

_____

_____

sculptured nail mistakes

You've reviewed what products are needed and the procedure steps, but there is still much more to remember for your state board exam. Answer **Yes** or **No** to these questions about common mistakes that can be made during the practical exam.

_____ 1. Should you do all the required prep for the natural nail even though it's only for one nail?

_____ 2. Should you apply pressure with the abrasive board when etching the natural nail?

_____ 3. Should you clean the model's nail before the application of the product?

_____ 4. Should any nail product to get on the model's cuticle area?

_____ 5. Should you leave oil on the natural nail before the application of the monomer liquid and polymer powder?

_____ 6. Do you need to practice with an odorless product before the exam to ensure your product dries correctly?

_____ 7. Should you blow or fan the nail in an attempt to hasten the drying time?

_____ 8. Should you clean your brush during the application to keep it free from hardened product?

_____ 9. Should you place the white bead on the end of the nail, rather than on the nail form?

_____ 10. Should you etch the natural nail by going across the nail from side to side?

state board sculpture nail practice exam

Find two students to partner with. Practice your state board tip and wrap application from nail prep to polish on your "student model." During the process have your "student examiner" check yes or no to the questions on the following page.

State Board One-Color Monomer Liquid And Polymer Powder Nail Practical Exam

nail prep

	YES	NO
1. Were the participant's hands washed?	☐	☐
2. Were the model's hands washed?	☐	☐
3. Was the required cuticle care properly performed?	☐	☐
4. Was the shine removed from the nail adequately and safely?	☐	☐
5. Was dust properly removed from the natural nail?	☐	☐
6. Were the oil and any residual products removed completely from the natural nail?	☐	☐
7. Was a nail dehydrator applied to the model's finger before the application of the monomer liquid and polymer powder?	☐	☐

one color monomer liquid and polymer powder nail enhancement

	YES	NO
8. Were the model's nails in compliance with the directions?	☐	☐
9. Were safety glasses and gloves applied before the application of primer?	☐	☐
10. Were the model's nails the correct length?	☐	☐
11. Was the nail form applied properly?	☐	☐
12. Were the nail products applied correctly?	☐	☐
13. Zone 1 performed first and correctly?	☐	☐
14. Zone 2 performed second and correctly?	☐	☐
15. Zone 3 performed last and correctly?	☐	☐
16. Were products kept away from the cuticle area?	☐	☐
17. Was the primer properly applied?	☐	☐
18. Was the final shaping of the nail adequate?	☐	☐
19. Were the cuticle area and sides of the finger free from damage while filing?	☐	☐

nail structure

	YES	NO
20. Was the apex/arch area in the center of the nail at the stress point?	☐	☐
21. Did the sidewalls extend straight off the natural nail line?	☐	☐
22. Was the underside of the nail smooth and free from glitches?	☐	☐
23. Was the thickness at the tip of the nail credit card thin?	☐	☐
24. Did the surface and bottom side of the c-curve match perfectly?	☐	☐
25. Was the extension length in balance with the natural nail?	☐	☐

overall

	YES	NO
26. Were all bottles/jars properly capped when not in use?	☐	☐
27. Were all implements and supplies disposed of properly?	☐	☐
28. Were all safety requirements observed?	☐	☐
29. Did the service flow smoothly without interruption?	☐	☐
30. Was the procedure completed within the allotted time frame?	☐	☐

All yes answers are worth 3.333 points. What is the score out of 100? ☐

chapter 17: monomer liquid and polymer powder review

Complete the multiple-choice questions below by circling the correct answer to each question.

1. Nearly all ingredients used for nail enhancements come from the _____ family.
   a. Monomer
   b. Polymer
   c. Acrylic
   d. None of the above

2. What makes up the majority of the liquid monomer product?
   a. Ethyl methacrylate monomer
   b. Methyl methacrylate monomer
   c. Acrylic monomer
   d. None of the above

3. What is the initiator in acrylic powder?
   a. Catalyst
   b. Benzoyl peroxide or BPO
   c. Methyl methacrylate or MMA
   d. B and C

4. The amount of monomer liquid and polymer powder used to create a bead is referred to as:
   a. Forming a bead
   b. Absorption rate
   c. Mix ratio
   d. A and C

5. A _____ bead is created from equal amounts of liquid and powder.
   a. Wet
   b. Medium
   c. Dry
   d. None of the above

6. Why is a nail enhancement dependent on having an appropriate mix ratio?
   a. For proper set
   b. For maximum durability
   c. For optimum workability
   d. All of the above

7. When too much powder is picked up in the bead, it can cause:
   a. Bubbles
   b. Brittleness
   c. Discoloration
   d. B and C

8. What product removes surface moisture and tiny amounts of oil left on the natural nail plate?
    a. Nail dehydrator
    b. Nail primer
    c. Product remover
    d. Non-acid primer

9. Nail forms are available in what type of material?
    a. Paper/mylar with adhesive backs
    b. Pre-shaped aluminum
    c. Pre-shaped plastic
    d. All of the above

10. What nail enhancement product can cause serious and sometimes irreversible damage to the skin and eyes?
    a. Monomer
    b. Acid-based nail primer
    c. Polymers
    d. Dehydrator

11. To obtain maximum shelf life, how should your nail adhesives be handled?
    a. Close the cap securely after each use.
    b. Set containers upright.
    c. Store between 60°F and 85°F.
    d. All of the above

12. What hair makes one of the best brush bristles for liquid and powder nail enhancements?
    a. Synthetic
    b. Sable
    c. Goat
    d. Human

13. A _____ grit is usually coarse enough to shape the nail enhancement.
    a. 100
    b. 150
    c. 180
    d. 220

14. How many hours does it take for a monomer liquid and polymer powder nail enhancement to reach ultimate strength?
    a. 1 to 2 hours
    b. 6 to 12 hours
    c. 12 to 24 hours
    d. 24 to 48 hours

15. For a more natural looking nail, the product near the _____ must be thin.
    a. Eponychium
    b. Side walls
    c. Free edge
    d. All of the above

Gina is scheduled for a two-color monomer liquid and polymer powder nail enhancement appointment. She had originally requested that you use forms to extend her nail length, so you have scheduled two hours for her service. When Gina arrives she tells you that she has to have a pedicure too, and she forgot to book it, but you have another client in exactly two hours. What can you do to accommodate Gina, and still manage to stay on time?

_____

_____

_____

_____

_____

_____

_____

_____

_____

18 uv gels

This chapter introduces UV gels, a type of nail enhancement product that hardens when exposed to a UV light. This has become an increasingly popular method for nail enhancement services recently, and a highly requested service in the salon. This product is not only applied very differently than what you have experienced so far, but it also is removed differently than the other enhancement products you have reviewed.

You will need to understand the difference between UV gel products and all overlay products before advising your clients on which type of nail enhancement will work best for them. So let's get started.

uv gel puzzle

Fill in the crossword puzzle with key words found in Chapter 18, by using the clues below.

ACROSS

1 Main ingredient used to create UV gel nail enhancements.

4 Two different colors of UV gel are applied to the surface of the nail, in different places, as in a French manicure.

6 The measurement of the thickness or thinness of a liquid that affects how the fluid flows.

8 Type of nail enhancement product that hardens when exposed to a UV light.

9 Measure of how much electricity a light bulb consumes.

11 Short chain of monomers that is not long enough to be considered a polymer.

12 The amount of pigment concentration in a UV gel making it difficult to see through.

DOWN

1 Main ingredient used to create latest UV gel technology.

2 Tacky surface left on the nail after a UV gel has cured.

3 A chemical that creates the polymerization reaction to begin when exposed to UV light.

5 UV gel is applied over the entire surface of the nail.

7 Specialized electronic device that powers and controls UV lamps to cure UV gel nail enhancements.

10 Special bulb that emits UV light to cure UV gel nail enhancements.

Fun Fact...

The same chemistry for UV gel nail products, using urethane acrylate, is a proven technology used worldwide for a broad range of applications. It's referred to as radiation curing, and is considered a "green" technology. Radiation curing has benefited from the trend away from environmentally unfriendly products such as solvent-based, thermally-cured coatings. Since many radiation curable coatings can cure in less than a second, they also quickly find their way to applications where continuous processing and high speeds are essential. Major industries are using this UV coating technology for goods such as hardwood and PVC flooring, wood and metal furniture, magazine covers, eyeglass lenses, mirrors, and coatings on plastic housings for cell phones and computers.

Source: http://www.specialchem4coatings.com/tc/radiation-curing

UV Gels

uv gel product and equipment facts

Answer True or False to the statements below about UV gel products, equipment, and how they are used.

T   F   **1.** When applying a UV gel enhancement, you must expose the nail to UV light after each layer of product is applied to the natural nail.

T   F   **2.** UV gel nails have a high odor problem.

T   F   **3.** As long as a UV light bulb displays blue light it will cure the enhancement.

T   F   **4.** When UV gel is exposed to UV light in its container, it will harden in the container.

T   F   **5.** Wattage indicates how much UV light is emitted from the UV light unit.

T   F   **6.** All UV lamps emit the same amount of UV rays.

T   F   **7.** UV gel enhancements rely on ingredients from the monomer and polymer chemical family

T   F   **8.** A UV light unit is a specialized electronic device that powers and controls UV lamps to cure UV gel nail enhancements

T   F   **9.** UV gel polish has a tendency to thicken over time because the solvents evaporate.

T   F   **10.** When removing the inhibition layer from the UV gel, avoid cleaning the nail in a manner that would put the UV gel onto the surface of the skin.

tools of the trade double puzzle

In addition to the materials required for a basic manicuring set-up, you will need other supplies and equipment to do a UV gel French overlay on a nail tip. Use the clues below to help you identify the special products and write your answer in the cells provided. Copy the letters in the numbered cells, to the cells with the same number to reveal the secret message!

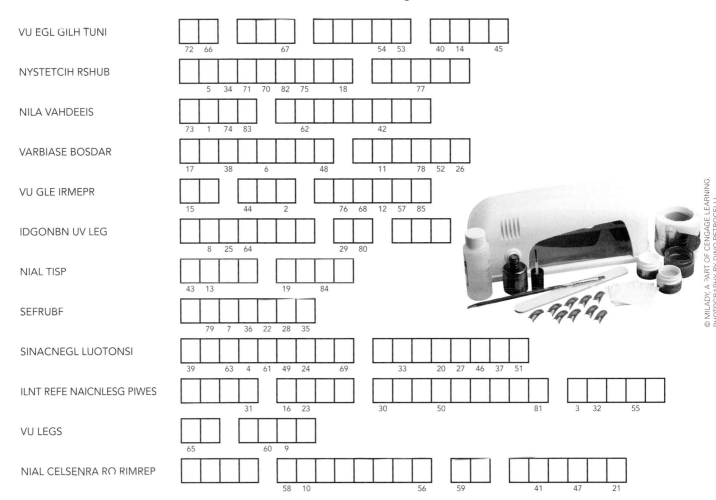

VU EGL GILH TUNI

72 66   67   54 53 40 14 45

NYSTETCIH RSHUB

5 34 71 70 82 75   18   77

NILA VAHDEEIS

73 1 74 83   62   42

VARBIASE BOSDAR

17 38 6   48   11 78 52 26

VU GLE IRMEPR

15 44 2   76 68 12 57 85

IDGONBN UV LEG

8 25 64   29 80

NIAL TISP

43 13   19 84

SEFRUBF

79 7 36 22 28 35

SINACNEGL LUOTONSI

39 63 4 61 49 24 69   33 20 27 46 37 51

ILNT REFE NAICNLESG PIWES

31 16 23   30 50 81   3 32 55

VU LEGS

65 60 9

NIAL CELSENRA RO RIMREP

58 10   56 59 41 47 21

© MILADY, A PART OF CENGAGE LEARNING. PHOTOGRAPHY BY DINO PETROCELLI.

Clues

1. Provides the UV light to cure the UV gel.
2. Used to apply UV gel to the nail.
3. Used for securing pre-formed nail tips to natural nails.
4. Used for shaping the enhancement.
5. Designed specifically to improve adhesion of UV gels to the natural nail plate.
6. Similar to a monomer and polymer primer, but will vary in consistency and chemical components.
7. Made from ABS plastic, to extend the nail length.
8. Used for smoothing the enhancement surface after filing.
9. An isopropanol solvent used to remove the inhibition layer.
10. Used to clean the nail with the solvent when removing the inhibition layer.
11. Includes the pink, white, clear and gloss UV gels needed for application.
12. Removes surface moisture and tiny amounts of oil left on the natural nail plate.

Secret Message:

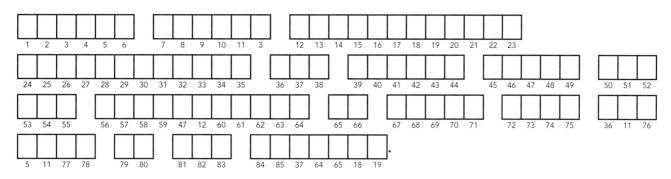

types of uv gels mini quiz

Describe the following types of UV gels and what they are used for in the spaces provided.

1. UV bonding gels

_____

2. UV building gels

_____

3. Self-leveling UVgels

_____

_____

4. Pigmented UV gels

_____

_____

_____

5. UV gel polishes

_____

_____

6. UV gloss gels

_____

uv gel polish application scramble

Unscramble the photos of the steps needed to create a UV gel polish nail enhancement service. Organize the steps by writing in a number from 1-14 according to which step starts first. Then write a description of what is happening in the photo.

Step _____

_____

_____

Step _____

_____

_____

Step _____

_____

_____

Step _____

_____

_____

Step _____

_____

_____

Step _____

_____

_____

Step _____

_____

_____

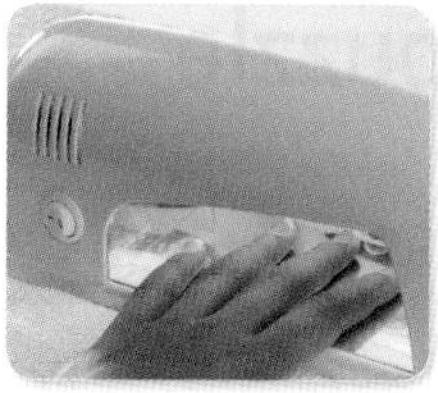

Step _____

_____

_____

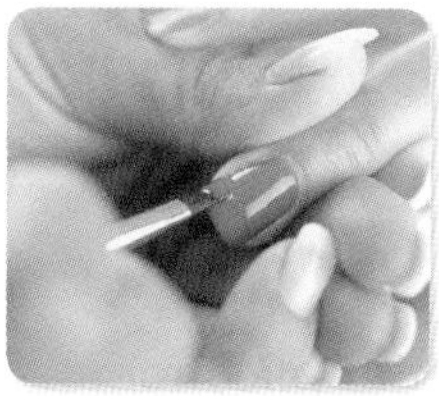

Step _____

_____

_____

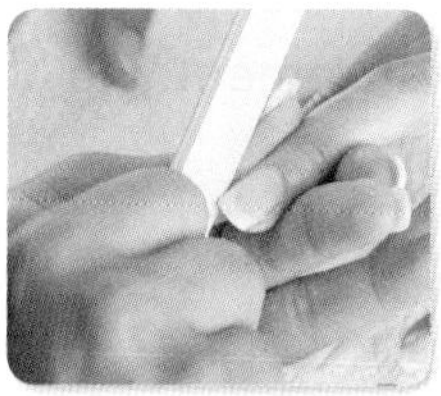

Step _____

_____

_____

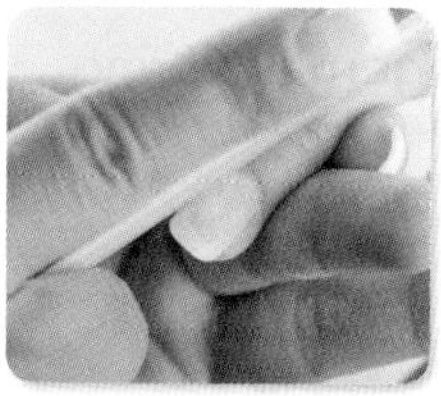

Step _____

_____

_____

Step _____

_____

_____

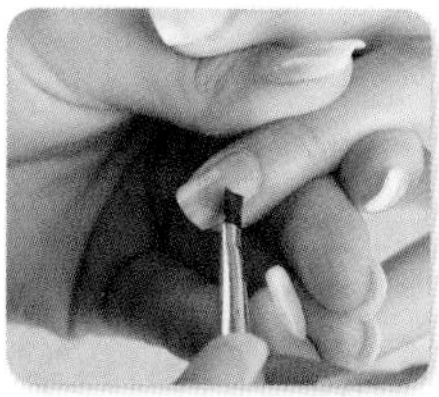

Step _____

_____

_____

Step _____

_____

_____

uv gels over monomer liquid and polymer powder puzzle

Fill in the blanks below to describe the steps for using UV gel over monomer liquid and polymer powder enhancements, then find your answers in the word find puzzle on the next page.

Tech Tip:

Some words are used more than once.

1. Perform _____ liquid and _____ powder application.

2. File, contour, _____, and _____ the enhancement. Do not use any _____ during this process.

3. Remove _____ and _____ with a cleaned and _____ nylon brush.

4. Remove any _____ that may have been deposited on the fingernail during filing.

5. Apply a _____ of _____ over the entire surface of the enhancement in a _____ technique.

6. Place the _____ inside the _____ and _____ for the recommended period of time.

7. Apply a thin coat of UV gel polish over the _____ surface.

8. Place the _____ inside the _____ and _____ for the recommended period of time.

9. Apply a _____ amount of the third UV gel which may be called _____ or _____ UV gel.

10. Cure _____ gel in UV light unit.

11. Remove the _____ layer, if required.

12. Apply nail _____.

13. Apply hand _____ and _____ hand and arm.

14. _____ nail enhancements.

```
E R M S H E S L T X H D S Y M
N S E A M G P H I S U E P S U
T K N M N O I A I O A T Q H E
I D F I O N O L H L I C C K X
R N L M C N O T E S F E M L F
E I H O I P O R H H Q F A L I
F Y A I L K Z M D E C N R A N
O T A E B N O I T O L I E M I
C I G G N I H S U R B S M S S
U V L I G H T U N I T I Y D H
U N V S S W S I K A V D L U I
L R B S E R U C O H J B O S N
P Z O S A Z J K W N B I P T G
X L C G M A S S A G E H O X V
G C L E A N D U A E Y V X Z N
```

Fun **Fact...**

Use the same procedure on toes as on fingernails!
The summer months call for the perfect pedicure,
and UV gel polish will do just that! There is no
chipping like traditional polish, and the shine won't
become dull!. This strong coating can also create
a perfect nail on an imperfect toenail, which could
create a loyal client base that requires routine maintenance, which equals a better income for you!

UV Gel Removal

There are two generally accepted methods of removing UV gels. One method involves hard UV gels (typically defined as the "traditional UV gels") and the other method involves soft UV gels. Read over the products needed and the removal steps below and in the space provided, indicate with SG if it's a product or step used to remove a soft UV gel or HG if it's a product or step to remove a hard UV gel.

Tech Tip:

Some steps will be used for both removal methods.

implements and materials

_____ Polish remover

_____ 180 grit file

_____ Nail Buffer

_____ UV gel remover (as recommended by the UV gel manufacturer)

_____ Glass bowl

_____ Wooden pusher

procedure steps

_____ Remove polish.

_____ Use an abrasive board to reduce the thickness of the enhancement.

_____ File the surface of the nail.

_____ Pour enough soak-off solution in the glass bowl to completely immerse the enhancements.

_____ Soak enhancements in solution for the time recommended by the manufacturer.

_____ Use a wooden stick or stainless steel pusher to ease the UV gel off the fingernail.

_____ Use a nail buffer to smooth the remaining enhancement for a natural shine.

_____ Lightly buff to remove any remaining UV gel material from the fingernail.

_____ Talk with the client about how to allow the rest of the enhancements to grow out and off of the fingernails.

_____ Suggest that your client have a series of natural nail manicures.

chapter 18: uv gel review

Complete the multiple-choice questions below by circling the correct answer to each question.

1. A UV lamp is a special _____ that emits UV light to cure UV gel nail enhancements.
   a. Machine
   b. Bulb
   c. Light
   d. Enclosure

2. If you do not change UV lamps on a regular basis, what do you risk?
   a. Service breakdown
   b. UV lamp shortage
   c. Skin irritation or sensitivity
   d. A and C

3. Most UV gels are made from:
   a. Acrylic
   b. Acrylates
   c. Methacrylates
   d. Methyl methacrylate

4. What would you use to remove the inhibition layer that is formed when UV gels harden?
   a. Acetone
   b. Benzoyl peroxide
   c. Alcohol
   d. A and C

5. UV gels rely on a related form of a monomer called:
   a. A polymer
   b. A primer
   c. An oligomer
   d. A and C

6. _____ is a special type of acrylate used in traditional UV gels.
   a. Urethane acrylate
   b. Poly acrylate
   c. Mono acyrlate
   d. None of the above

7. Depending on frequency of use, UV lamps should be changed out:
   a. Once a month
   b. Twice a month
   c. Two to three times a year
   d. When they burn out

8. What is the shelf life of nail adhesive?
   a. About a month
   b. About three months
   c. About six months
   d. About a year

9. What is the most common UV lamp on the market?
   a. 4-watt
   b. 6-watt
   c. 7-watt
   d. 9-watt

10. Newer UV gel technologies use:
    a. Methacrylates
    b. Acrylic
    c. Methyl methacrylate
    d. Urethane acrylate

11. Oligomers usually have a _____ consistency.
    a. Thick
    b. Gel-like
    c. Sticky
    d. All of the above

12. How long should each layer of the UV gel should be cured?
    a. 2 minutes
    b. For as long as the client is comfortable
    c. 3 minutes
    d. For as long as recommended by the manufacturer

13. Your UV gel and brush should be kept away from _____ during the application process to prevent the product from prematurely hardening.
    a. Incandescent light
    b. Direct sunlight
    c. Full-spectrum lighting
    d. B and C

14. You must rebalance UV gels every:
    a. 1 to 2 weeks
    b. 2 to 3 weeks
    c. 3 to 4 weeks
    d. Month

15. The difference between one light unit and another may be:
    a. The number of lamps in the unit
    b. The distance the lamps are from the bottom of the unit
    c. The size of the unit
    d. All of the above

Your client Tanya has been wearing tips with a UV gel overlay consistently for about eight months. She usually has a rebalance every three weeks. Yesterday, Tanya called to let you know that a few days after her last rebalance she had terrible itching around her cuticles and some redness as well. Although the redness and itching have stopped, she is worried about continuing to wear her nail enhancements.

What could you do to reassure Tanya that the service is safe and to prevent her from canceling all future appointments?

_____

_____

_____

_____

_____

_____

_____

_____

_____

_____

_____

_____

_____

_____

19 the creative touch

Welcome to the nail art chapter of the workbook! We're going to do some review, play some games, create some art and have a little fun. Ready? Good, let's get started!

nail art key words puzzle

Fill in the crossword puzzle with key words found in chapter 19, by using the clues below.

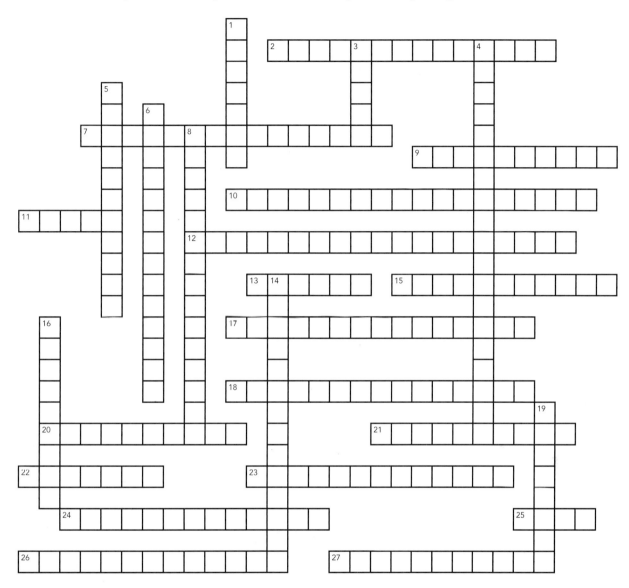

ACROSS

2 Nail art technique where the nail bed is one color, usually pink, peach, or beige (depending upon the client's skin tone), and the free edge of the nail is another color, usually white.

7 Colors resulting from mixing equal parts of two primary colors; the positions opposite to the primary colors on a color wheel.

9 Description used for nail art when more than one nail art medium is used to create the design.

10 Information provided for each competition so that one understands what the competition allows and does not allow.

11 Any art that protrudes from the nail.

12 Opportunities for licensed professionals or nail students to compete in a specified category where the art and or theme of the nails are part of the judging criteria.

13 Tool with a solid handle and a rounded ball tip on each end that can range in size.

15 When one color fades into the other, and the meeting point is a combination of the two.

17 A pre-cut sheet of clear, thin plastic with a sticky backing that is cut by a machine into various shapes or designs.

18 Colors that are located beside each other on the color wheel.

20 A color guide that illustrates and identifies the primary, secondary, tertiary, and complementary colors.

21 Nail art category or competition where all art mediums are allowed and the only limitation is the imagination.

22 Fed / Airbrush system designed to pull the paint into the airbrush using gravity

23 Creating blocks or sections of color on the nail.

24 Pure pigment colors that cannot be obtained from mixing together other colors.

25 When UV gel or other product settles and flattens out while working.

26 Designs inside a nail enhancement that are created when nail art is sandwiched between two layers of product while the nail enhancement is being formed.

27 A swirled effect when you combine two or more colors together when wet and mix them on the nail with a marbleizing tool known as a stylus.

DOWN

1 A nail art category that includes all freehand painting techniques that are flat, not raised.

3 The light we see reflected from a surface.

4 Colors located directly opposite each other on the color wheel.

5 A competition where you may use pink, white clear, and glittered products to produce a unique twist on the French look.

6 A kit you must take with you of all products you will use or might use in the competition.

8 Sculptured nail enhancements that have inlaid designs and are produced using either monomer liquid and polymer powder or UV gel products.

14 Colors resulting from mixing equal parts of one primary color and one of its nearest secondary colors.

16 Placing wet UV gel product under the UV light for 5-10 seconds.

19 Usually 15-30 minutes before the start of the competition, when the competition director or head judge will review the rules and guidelines to ensure everyone understands and is able to comply.

Getting The Look: Art Mediums

french manicure practice

Since the French manicure is the most popular nail art service in the nail salon today, you'll likely be doing lots and lots of them—so mastering the "smile line" is a must! Remember that a smile line can be accomplished with polish, paint, monomer liquid and polymer powder, and UV gel products, and smile lines will appear more dramatic on some nails than others depending on the nail bed length, the free edge length and the client's preferences. To be competitive in the market, you will certainly want your smile lines to be gorgeous, and one way to do this is to practice and another is to envision how the final nail will look before you start.

draw this!

Below is an example of four different styles of nail beds. With a pencil, draw in the French manicure smile line and free edge length. Remember to be consistent with the smile line on every set, and create a beautiful balance with the length of the free edge. Hint: always start with the irregular or shortest nail bed first to determine the degree of smile line and then stay consistent with the other nails.

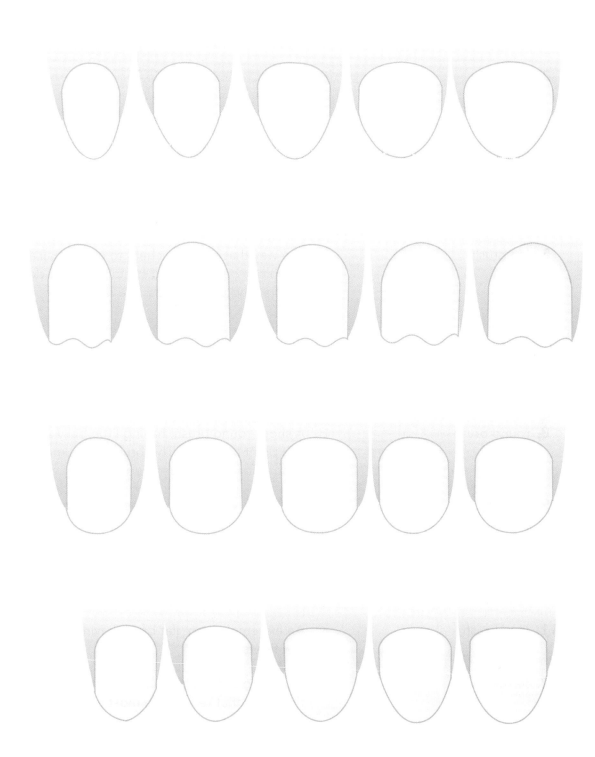

Paint

tools of the trade

Match the following paint brushes and brush terms with their descriptions or uses.

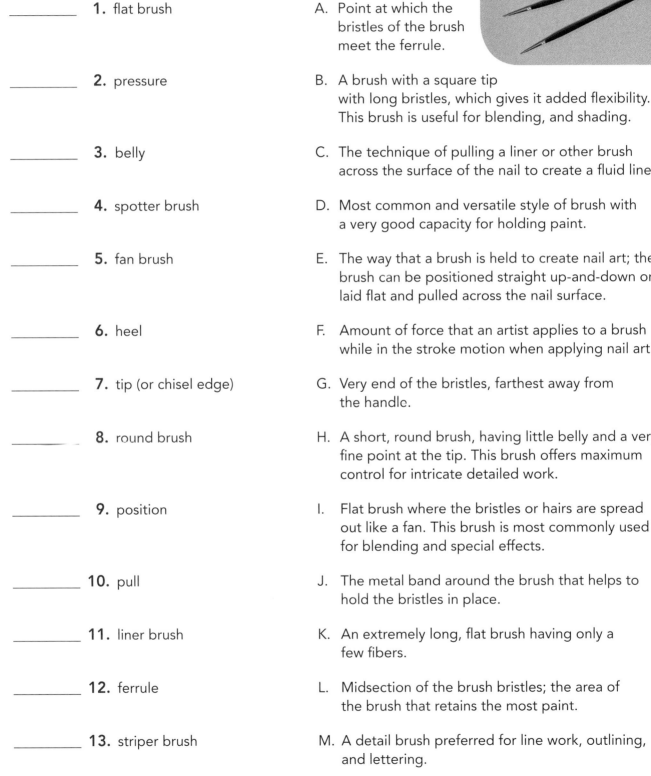

_____ **1.** flat brush

A. Point at which the bristles of the brush meet the ferrule.

_____ **2.** pressure

B. A brush with a square tip with long bristles, which gives it added flexibility. This brush is useful for blending, and shading.

_____ **3.** belly

C. The technique of pulling a liner or other brush across the surface of the nail to create a fluid line.

_____ **4.** spotter brush

D. Most common and versatile style of brush with a very good capacity for holding paint.

_____ **5.** fan brush

E. The way that a brush is held to create nail art; the brush can be positioned straight up-and-down or laid flat and pulled across the nail surface.

_____ **6.** heel

F. Amount of force that an artist applies to a brush while in the stroke motion when applying nail art.

_____ **7.** tip (or chisel edge)

G. Very end of the bristles, farthest away from the handle.

_____ **8.** round brush

H. A short, round brush, having little belly and a very fine point at the tip. This brush offers maximum control for intricate detailed work.

_____ **9.** position

I. Flat brush where the bristles or hairs are spread out like a fan. This brush is most commonly used for blending and special effects.

_____ **10.** pull

J. The metal band around the brush that helps to hold the bristles in place.

_____ **11.** liner brush

K. An extremely long, flat brush having only a few fibers.

_____ **12.** ferrule

L. Midsection of the brush bristles; the area of the brush that retains the most paint.

_____ **13.** striper brush

M. A detail brush preferred for line work, outlining, and lettering.

Fun Fact...

Nail art can be addictive, so offer a free sample to your client when time allows. If she loves it, she will most likely request it again at her next service, increasing your profits!

practice time!

SUPPLIES: You will need to use a standard, clear sheet protector to perform this exercise. The sheet protector will be considered your "practice window." You also have the option of laminating this page to keep for a long time.

Cover the area below with your "practice window" and practice the brush strokes shown using your nail art brushes and paints. Try each stroke at least 10 times.

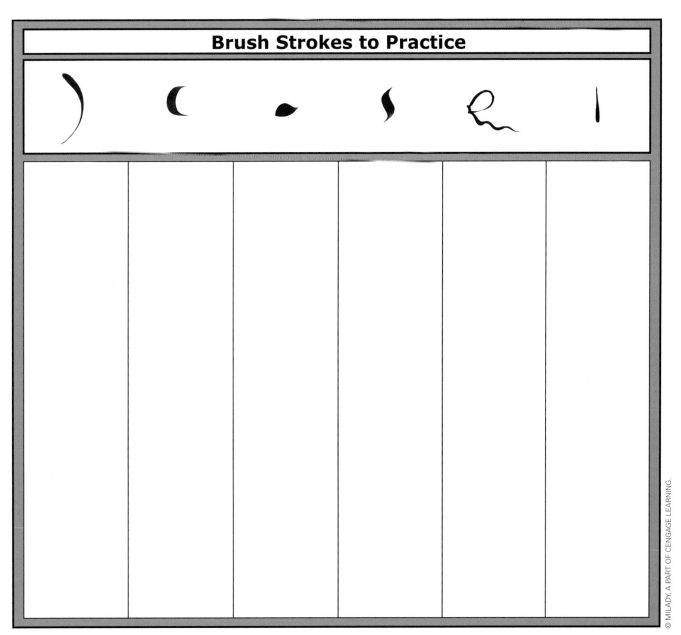

Brush Strokes to Practice

nail art mini quiz

Fill in the blanks to answer these questions about using monomer liquid and polymer powder to create nail art.

1. What five products/supplies will you need to create 3D art using monomer liquid and polymer powder?

   _____

   _____

   _____

   _____

2. 3D art can be used over what products?

   _____

   _____

3. Name at least three ways monomer liquid and polymer powder can be used to create nail art.

   _____

   _____

4. Describe the perfect bead.

   _____

   _____

5. What do you have to be careful not to do when using this medium over polish?

   _____

   _____

   _____

practice time!

SUPPLIES: You will need to use a standard, clear sheet protector to perform this exercise. The sheet protector will be considered your "practice window." You also have the option of laminating this page to keep for a long time.

Cover the grid lines below with your practice window and follow the directions given to practice monomer liquid and polymer powder beads for nail art.

Test 1: Learn how the product behaves by trying the activity below.

1. Place a small bead of product on the grid. Notice how it sinks or spreads out.

2. Using less liquid in your brush, place another bead of the same size on the grid. Notice how much it sinks or spreads out now.

3. Try picking up the same size bead and dabbing the excess liquid off your brush onto your lint free absorbent towel. Now place that bead on the grid and notice how much it spreads out.

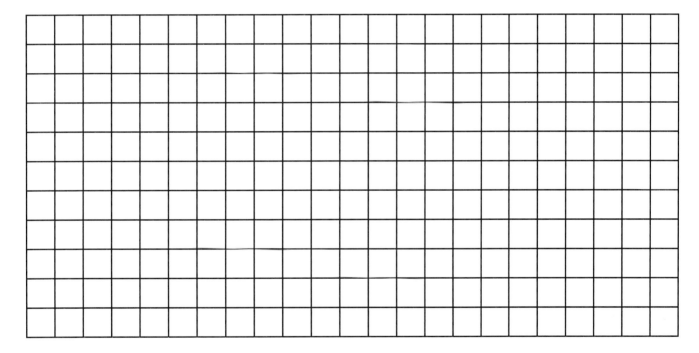

Tech Tip:

Each bead should sink or spread out less and less. The less monomer liquid you use, the more firm the bead will be, allowing you the product control to create raised 3D designs.

Test 2: Remove all product from your practice window and follow the steps below to create product control.

1. Create a very tiny dry bead and place it on the cross-lines of the grid below.

2. Repeat this 10 times, trying to keep all the beads the same size and shape.

3. Create the same tiny dry bead of product, place it on the cross-lines of the grid.

4. Bring your brush to a point by pulling it across your lint free absorbent towel.

5. Place the tip of your brush at the edge of the bead and lean your brush back to flatten and open the bead inside the square like a petal. Try not to make the petal much bigger than the square box.

6. Repeat step five 10 times, trying to create the same size beads and flattening them to fill a square box.

7. Try repeating steps 3-5 using a little larger bead. Notice how the "petals" are the same size as the previous petals, but that they are much thicker.

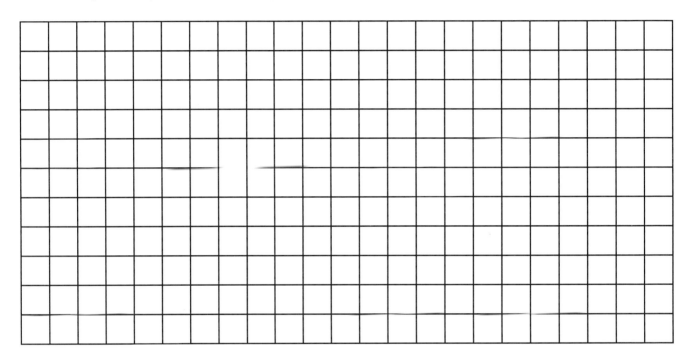

Tech **Tip:**

The bigger and dryer the bead, the thicker or more 3D the petal. As you practice this, the beads should become more consistent in size and shape. You will learn to understand what size bead to use for nail art depending on the results you are trying to achieve.

Fun **Fact...**

Create your own custom colored powders for nail art by grinding small amounts of powder pigments with your polymer powders. Use pigment with clear polymer powders for transparent color or with white polymer powder to create opaque colors.

confetti inlaid design steps

On the lines below each picture, describe what's happening in the procedure for creating an inlaid design using confetti and UV gel over a clear tip.

© MILADY, A PART OF CENGAGE LEARNING. PHOTOGRAPHY BY DINO PETROCELLI.

_____
_____
_____
_____
_____
_____

© MILADY, A PART OF CENGAGE LEARNING. PHOTOGRAPHY BY DINO PETROCELLI.

_____
_____
_____
_____
_____
_____

© MILADY, A PART OF CENGAGE LEARNING. PHOTOGRAPHY BY DINO PETROCELLI.

_____
_____
_____
_____
_____
_____

© MILADY, A PART OF CENGAGE LEARNING. PHOTOGRAPHY BY DINO PETROCELLI.

_____
_____
_____
_____
_____
_____

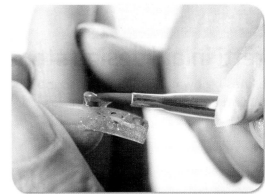

_____

_____

_____

_____

_____

_____

_____

_____

_____

_____

Fun **Fact...**

Any nail art that can be done on fingers can also be done on toes. Don't forget to suggest nail art during your pedicure services.

_____

_____

_____

_____

_____

_____

_____

_____

Embellishments

all about embellishments double puzzle!

Unscramble the embellishments listed below and write the word inside the cells. Copy the letters in the numbered cells to the other cells with the same number to reveal the secret message!

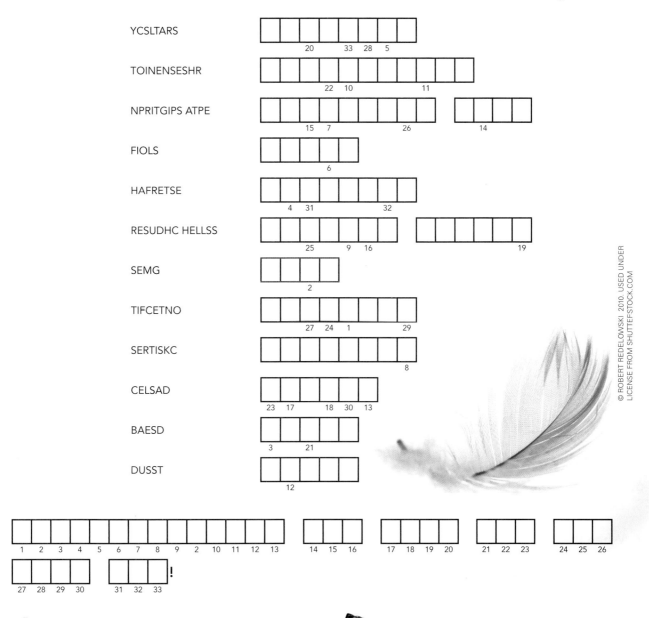

YCSLTARS
    20 33 28 5

TOINENSESHR
    22 10   11

NPRITGIPS ATPE
    15 7   26   14

FIOLS
    6

HAFRETSE
    4 31   32

RESUDHC HELLSS
    25 9 16   19

SEMG
    2

TIFCETNO
    27 24 1   29

SERTISKC
    8

CELSAD
    23 17   18 30 13

BAESD
    3   21

DUSST
    12

1 2 3 4 5 6 7 8 9 2 10 11 12 13 14 15 16 17 18 19 20 21 22 23 24 25 26

27 28 29 30 31 32 33 !

Fun **Fact...**

Even in 1100 B.C. the Chinese enjoyed the look of nail art! Gold, jewel-adorned nail guards were worn to protect against damaging their long, natural nails.

airbrushing machine and supplies

Using the words provided, fill in the blanks below to complete these statements about how airbrushing machines work and their supplies.

absorbent paper	cap	handle	overspray
air	cleaningcontainer	jar	paint
airbrush cleaner	color cup	mask knife	paper towels
airbrush stencil	compressor	mask paper	trigger
air hose	fluid nozzle	moisture trap	water
bowl	gravity-fed	needle	well

1. All airbrushes work on the same principle; they combine _____ and _____ to form an atomized spray, which releases extremely tiny droplets that are spray-painted on to the nails.

2. The ideal airbrush systems for nail art are designed for _____ painting, which uses gravity to pull the _____ into the airbrush.

3. All airbrush machines consist of three basic parts: the _____, _____ and _____.

4. The airbrush handle consists of the _____, _____, _____, _____ and paint _____ or cup.

5. At the tip or end of the airbrush handle, there is a small cone-shaped _____ _____ that a tapered _____ fits into.

6. The farther the _____ is drawn back, the more _____ that is allowed to come through the opening.

7. When the _____ is pressed and the _____ is drawn back, the airbrush begins to release paint.

8. A _____, also called a reservoir, is a hole in the top of the airbrush, where drops of paint are placed.

9. If the airbrush has a _____, it may be located on top of the airbrush or it may be attached to the side of the airbrush for holding _____.

10. The _____ attaches to the handle and will connect to the _____.

11. When you begin airbrushing, you will want to set up a cleaning area off to the side of the work area that may consist of a _____ or _____ lined with absorbent material like _____. You will use this container to spray out left-over paint and clean the handle after each color used.

12. When the compressed air reaches the _____, moisture can accumulate. You may want to purchase a _____ to prevent water droplets from spitting out of the airbrush.

13. Begin practicing on _____, or _____.

14. To clean the airbrush of color, you will want to remove the _____ or _____ and finish spraying all the paint from the handle into the _____.

15. Once all the color is gone and only air is coming out of the tip, add a couple drops of _____ or _____ to the well and continue to spray until only air is coming out of the tip.

16. You will always want to cover the working area with _____ or _____ to catch the _____.

17. To create designs or specific shapes when airbrushing, you can use a commercially prepared _____.

18. You can create a custom shape or designs with sheets of un-cut _____ and cut it yourself using a _____.

Fun Fact...

If you wear it, they will come. Your hands are the billboards to your business. Wear your nail art and your bank teller, grocery checker, and the girl who makes your double-shot caramel latte will notice it. Everyone needs to know YOU DO NAILS, and this is just the conversation starter. Be sure to have plenty of business cards on hand, and a 10 percent discount stamped on the back doesn't hurt either.

-10%

The Business Of Nail Art

practice this!

In the salon, time is money! So, it's important to create beautiful nail art in a reasonable amount of time. How can you do this? Practice, practice, practice! Practicing the art will not only help you create more consistent and beautiful designs, but it also will allow you to increase speed.

Choose five different nail art techniques that you like. You may want to stick with one art medium for this exercise, like polish art. Time yourself while creating the nail art on a nail tip. Then try each two more times. Record your progress in the chart below.

Nail Art Timed Progress			
	Record time in minutes for one nail.		
Nail Art Description	1st	2nd	3rd

Nail Art Competitions!

competition facts

Circle true or false about the facts given below about nail art competitions.

T   F   **1.** Nail competitions are very popular and prestigious events in the nail industry.

T   F   **2.** Nail art competitions create opportunities for everyone to compete in a specified category where the art and or theme of the nails are part of the judging criteria.

T   F   **3.** Rules and guidelines are provided for each competition so that one understands what the competition allows and does not allow.

T   F   **4.** There are novice and veteran competitions, student and professional categories, and sometimes levels of competition experience are a factor in entering a category.

T   F   **5.** After finding out the rules, guidelines, and location of the competition you want to enter, you will only need to show up on time at the venue to participate.

T   F   **6.** There are on-line and photo competitions which are a reasonably stress-free way to try your hand at competing.

T   F   **7.** Trade shows are a vital part of our industry and an important platform for nail professionals to recruit new salon clients.

T　F　**8.** Putting your nail art on display for your peers will give you invaluable feedback on | where you need to improve, and where you stand in comparison to the highest standards of the industry.

T　F　**9.** Creating a competition kit will mean listing every product you will or might use and packing it to take to the competition.

T　F　**10.** The briefing usually occurs the day before the competition when the competition director or head judge will review the rules and guidelines to ensure everyone understands them and is able to comply.

T　F　**11.** Flat art is a nail art category that includes all free-hand painting techniques that are flat, not raised.

T　F　**12.** In 3D art competitions, most embellishments are allowed, and most other artwork is created using UV gel, as this medium is easiest to work with in making 3-D art.

T　F　**13.** Design sculpture nails are when a 3D design is sculpted on top of the nail enhancement.

T　F　**14.** For a French twist competition, you may use pink, white, clear, and glittered products to produce a traditional French manicured look.

T　F　**15.** Airbrushed art may be done prior and presented in a box, or done on a model with a full set of nails on, in a timed competition.

T　F　**16.** The term mixed media is a description used for nail art when one nail art medium is used and a mixed design is created.

T　F　**17.** Most competitors spend between 15 to 30 minutes to produce a fantasy art display for competition.

chapter 19: the creative touch review

Complete the multiple-choice questions below by circling the correct answer to each question.

1. A client may become interested in nail art by seeing a display or example. Which of the following are ways of displaying nail art?
   a. On tips in a glass case or frame
   b. In a photo gallery or portfolio
   c. On your own nails
   d. All of the above

2. What type of nails can nail art be displayed on?
   a. Polished natural nails
   b. Polished toe nails
   c. Artificial nail enhancements
   d. All of the above

3. What should you remember when introducing nail art to your clients?
   a. Amount of time it takes to complete the art
   b. Services they usually have
   c. Implements, tools, and supplies needed
   d. A and C

4. What color would be an example of a secondary color?
   a. Orange
   b. Red
   c. Blue
   d. Black

5. What is an example of a primary color?
   a. White
   b. Red
   c. Green
   d. Violet

6. Tertiary colors are sometimes referred to as what?
   a. Complementary colors
   b. Intermediate colors
   c. Bright colors
   d. None of the above

7. What colors are located directly opposite each other on the color wheel?
   a. Complementary colors
   b. Tertiary colors
   c. Intermediate colors
   d. None of the above

8. What colors are located beside each other on the color wheel?
   a. Complementary colors
   b. Tertiary colors
   c. Intermediate colors
   d. None of the above

9. What type of nail art look is created when two colors are swirled together when wet?
   a. Color graduation
   b. Marbleizing
   c. Color blocking
   d. French manicure

10. What basic technique should you master when practicing brush strokes for hand-painted nail art?
    a. Pressure
    b. Comma
    c. C stroke
    d. S stroke

11. What type of nail art can be achieved when using monomer liquid and polymer powder products?
    a. 3D
    b. Inlaid designs
    c. French manicure
    d. All the above

12. What type of products can be sandwiched between two layers of enhancement products to form an inlaid design?
    a. Monomer liquid and polymer powder
    b. UV gel
    c. Embellishments
    d. All of the above

13. What art mediums can be used to create a color fade or color graduation?
    a. Polish
    b. Monomer liquid and polymer powder
    c. Airbrushing
    d. All of the above

14. When creating nail art with monomer liquid and polymer powder, what should the perfect bead look like?
    a. White and shiny
    b. Dry and smooth
    c. Smooth and shiny
    d. Creamy and glossy

15. What type of art medium can create a French manicure look?
    a. Polish
    b. Paint
    c. UV gel
    d. All of the above

16. When applying 3D nail art over polish with monomer liquid and polymer powder, how long should you wait after you have completed polishing the nails?
    a. No wait time needed, apply 3D art immediately
    b. Wait at least 3 minutes
    c. Wait at least 10 minutes
    d. None of the above

17. When creating inlaid designs, you must ensure that the art inside the nail is:
    a. Shiny
    b. Clear
    c. Thin
    d. Colorful

18. What are you trying to avoid by flash curing UV gel?
    a. Bubbles
    b. Sinking
    c. Swirling
    d. A and B

19. What type of nail art can be done on toe nails?
    a. Paint
    b. Embellishments
    c. UV gel
    d. All of the above

20. What are the three basic parts of an airbrush system?
    a. Fluid nozzle, needle, and hose
    b. Handle, air hose and compressor
    c. Trigger, color cup and compressor
    d. Handle, trigger, and needle

21. An airbrush usually has what for holding the paint?
    a. Paint handle
    b. Well
    c. Fluid nozzle
    d. Color cap

22. What does airbrush paint look like on the nail if correctly applied?
    a. Dull with a powdery look
    b. Shiny with a high gloss finish
    c. Tiny droplets or puddles
    d. None of the above

23. To create the perfect depth of color when airbrushing, you must:
    a. Spray continuously until the color appears
    b. Spray with a darker color then what you will want
    c. Spray the color light, wait a few minutes and repeat
    d. None of the above

24. Where would you find information about nail art competitions?
    a. Nail magazines
    b. Nail salons
    c. Nail industry websites
    d. A and C

25. Why would you or other nail technicians want to compete in a nail art competition?
    a. Inspiration and motivation
    b. Networking with peers
    c. Respect
    d. A and B

what would you do? a salon scenario

It's a hot summer day and your client just left. You check your schedule and learn that Rita is coming in for a spa manicure at 2:00 pm and you don't have another booking until 3:30 pm. This leaves about 30-45 minutes down time between these clients. Rita has shown interest in your nail art samples, but has never tried it. What would you do to introduce Rita to an add-on nail art service and when would be the appropriate time for this suggestion? How would you get Rita to at least try some nail art before she left the salon?

_____

_____

_____

_____

_____

_____

_____

_____

_____

Part4

BUSINESS SKILLS

20

seeking
employment

To be successful in the nail business, you will need to use your time wisely, plan for the future, go the extra mile, and draw on a reservoir of self-confidence to meet any challenge. Everyone wants to be successful, but what can you do to plan for your success? Most successful professionals will advise you to become self-motivated, be energetic and persistent, find a mentor and a supportive network of people—so you have plenty of resources to fall back on when challenges do arise. If you want to enjoy professional freedom, artistic expression and a successful career—start to plan for it now, because plenty of opportunities to make your dreams come true await you!

employment tools and tips double puzzle

Use the clues below to help you identify the tools and tips that will assist you in looking for and finding a job as a nail technician. Write your answer inside the cells and then copy the letters in the numbered cells to the cells with the same number to reveal the secret message!

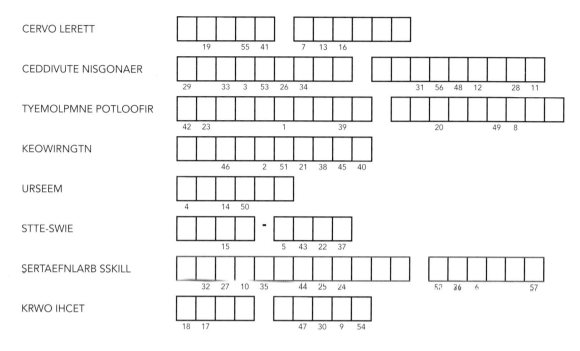

CERVO LERETT — 19 55 41 / 7 13 16

CEDDIVUTE NISGONAER — 29 33 3 53 26 34 / 31 56 48 12 28 11

TYEMOLPMNE POTLOOFIR — 42 23 1 39 / 20 49 8

KEOWIRNGTN — 46 2 51 21 38 45 40

URSEEM — 4 14 50

STTE-SWIE — 15 - 5 43 22 37

SERTAEFNLARB SSKILL — 32 27 10 35 44 25 24 / 52 36 6 57

KRWO IHCET — 18 17 / 47 30 9 54

Clues

1. Letter of introduction that highlights your goals, skills, and accomplishments.
2. Process of reaching logical conclusions by employing logical reasoning.
3. Collection of photographs and documents that reflect a person's skills, accomplishments, and abilities in a chosen career field.
4. Establishing contacts that may eventually lead to a job and that help you gain valuable information about the workings of various establishments.
5. Written summary of a person's education and work experience.
6. Having a complete and thorough knowledge of the subject matter, and understanding the strategies for taking tests successfully.
7. Skills mastered at other jobs that can be put to use in a new position.
8. Taking pride in your work, committing yourself consistently, and doing a good job for your clients, employer, and salon team.

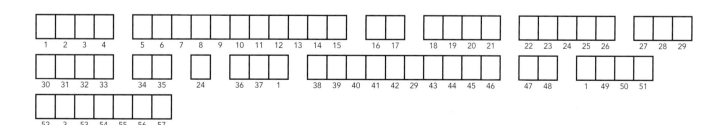

Preparing For Licensure

Fill in the blanks in the three sections below to complete the tips that will better prepare you for the written and practical licensing examination. Then find your answers in the word find puzzle.

written exam study habits

1. Keep well-organized _____ and _____.

2. Develop a _____ list.

3. Take effective _____ during class.

4. _____ information by listening and asking questions.

5. _____ past quizzes and tests.

6. Develop a _____ toward taking the test.

written test day strategies

7. Get plenty of _____ the night before the test.

8. Dress _____.

9. Anticipate some _____; feeling concerned about the test results may actually help you do better.

10. Arrive _____ with a self-confident attitude; be alert, calm, and ready for the challenge.

11. Know exactly where you are going and how to get there _____ the day of the exam.

12. Read all written directions, and _____ carefully to all verbal directions before beginning.

13. Wear a _____ to budget your time to ensure that you have plenty of opportunity to complete the test.

14. Answer the _____ questions first in order to save time for the more difficult ones. Quickly scanning all the questions first may give you an idea about which questions are more difficult.

15. Answer as many questions as possible. If you are unsure about some questions, _____ or _____. Do not spend too much time on any one question.

16. Mark the questions you _____ so that you can find them again later.

practical exam preparation tips

17. _____ the correct skills required in the test as often as you can.

18. Participate in _____ licensing examinations, including the _____ of the examination criteria.

19. Familiarize yourself with the _____ contained in the examination bulletins sent by the licensing agency.

20. Make certain that all equipment and _____ are cleaned, disinfected, and in good working order before the exam.

21. Bring extra _____ and alternate _____, implements, and equipment.

22. If allowed by the regulatory or licensing agency, _____ other practical examinations before taking your exam.

23. As with any exam, _____ carefully to the examiner's _____ and follow them explicitly.

24. Focus on your own _____; do not allow yourself to be concerned with what other test _____ are doing.

25. Follow all _____ and _____ procedures throughout the entire examination.

```
E E R P V P E K O S S S Z N E R H E C T
I D S E T O N G Y T R U O T T N T T L I
T M U F P U U X D J A P P J S A F S A M
P N P T S K O O B E T O N P M N A T R I
T C E L I N T O R D L M D I L F V S I N
S A L T E T N Q O E O W T C E I S B F G
B N S I N M T D Y C S S O T V E E Y Y H
S D T P S O E A K W E T Y N U I G S K K
N I U S W T C N E H S T K G K E U Y P Q
O D O K E V E I T V V O C A B U L A R Y
I A D I J Z V N I S I B C Y N B R Y J J
T T N P X E D Y A I A T I V A T O O L S
C E A A R K J N L H U L I T B E F O R E
U S H I Y F I H T R D R R S G N M F A E
R P R A C T I C E K A O Z Q O O F N J V
T K R U A A I T F H F E K T Q P X K G R
S V P T E H E A Q M B T T S E I S A E E
N M I Z L O L W O V X R C N E H H A K S
I O S Z J P W C K L E Q V T I N X J Y B
C L E A N I N G W K R S Y D P U E U V O
```

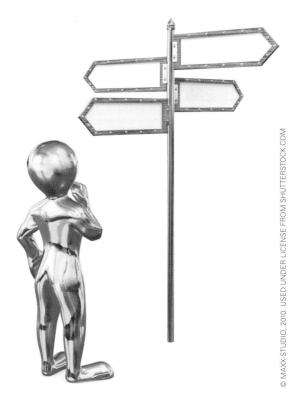

Fun **Fact...**

Employers are not allowed to discriminate because an applicant is not a U.S. citizen; however, upon request, you must be able to provide proof that you are legally in the U.S. and are allowed to work.

© MAXX-STUDIO, 2010. USED UNDER LICENSE FROM SHUTTERSTOCK.COM

Preparing For Employment

setting personal goals

Fill in the two forms below, and then use that information to answer the three questions below to help you reaffirm your career goals.

INVENTORY OF PERSONAL CHARACTERISTICS

PERSONAL CHARACTERISTICS	EXC.	GOOD	AVG.	POOR	PLAN FOR IMPROVEMENT
Posture, Deportment, Poise					
Image, Grooming, Personal Hygiene					
Etiquette, Manners, Courtesy					
Communications Skills					
Personality, Attitude					
Goals, Self-Motivation					
Personal Habits, Procrastination					
Responsibility					
Self-esteem, Self Confidence					
Integrity, Honesty					
Dependability, Loyalty					

© MILADY, A PART OF CENGAGE LEARNING.

INVENTORY OF TECHNICAL SKILLS

TECHNICAL SKILLS	EXC.	GOOD	AVG.	POOR	PLAN FOR IMPROVEMENT
Manicures, Hand/Arm Massage					
Pedicures, Foot Massage					
Polish Applications					
Hand Filing, Electric Filing					
Nail Tip and Nail Form Applications					
Fabric Wrap Application					
UV Gel Application					
Monomer Liquid and Polymer Powder Nail Enhancements Application					
Nail Art					
Paraffin Wax Treatments					

1. What do you really want out of a career in nail technology?

_____

_____

_____

_____

2. What areas within the nail industry are most interesting to you?

_____

_____

_____

_____

3. What are your strongest practical skills and in what ways do you wish to use them?

_____

_____

_____

_____

salon choices mini quiz

In the space provided, describe the salon business and opportunities available at these different types of salon businesses.

1. Small Independent Salons

_____

_____

_____

_____

_____

_____

2. Independent Salon Chains

_____

_____

_____

_____

_____

_____

3. Large National Salon Chains

_____

_____

_____

_____

_____

_____

4. Franchise Salons

_____

_____

_____

_____

_____

_____

5. Basic Value-Priced Operations

_____

_____

_____

_____

_____

_____

_____

6. Mid-Priced Full-Service Salons

_____

_____

_____

_____

_____

_____

_____

7. High-End Salons or Day Spas

_____

_____

_____

_____

_____

_____

_____

8. Booth Rental Establishments

_____

_____

_____

_____

_____

9. Which of these salons do you think will be best for you to work in when you get out of school?

_____

_____

_____

_____

_____

_____

10. Do you think you will be in this same salon in five years? Why?

_____

_____

_____

_____

_____

_____

_____

Resume And Employment Portfolio Development

resume guideline facts

A resume tells potential employers what your achievements and accomplishments are. Answer true or false to these basic guidelines for preparing your professional resume.

T F 1. Market yourself in such a manner that the reader will want to meet you.

T F 2. Keep it short. Ideally your resumé should be two to three pages.

T F 3. Always include a cover letter that introduces and highlights your goals, skills, and accomplishments.

T F 4. Learn to write a cover letter by researching books at public libraries or in bookstores.

T F 5. Print resumés and cover letters on good quality bond paper in any color that matches your personality.

T F 6. Include your name, address, phone number, and e-mail address only on the resumé and not your cover letter.

T F 7. Focus on information that is relevant to the position you are seeking.

T F 8. List all work experience you've ever had.

T F 9. List relevant education and the name of the institution from which you graduated, as well as relevant courses attended.

T F 10. List your abilities and accomplishments.

practice this!

Create the tools below that will assist you in searching for employment as a nail technician. Remember that you will use these tools in the next months while trying to secure a job, so be sure to research the proper formats for your cover letter and resume on the internet, at a library, or bookstore and create the documents on the proper resume paper. Preparing these tools perfectly now will ensure you are prepared when you are ready to apply for a position!

1. **Write a Cover Letter.** Look up a local salon you would consider as a prospect for employment and write a cover letter to the salon manager or owner.

2. **Create a Resume.** Develop a resume, as though you have graduated from nail school, using the tips for preparing a resume located in Chapter 20 of your textbook.

3. **Assemble an Employment Portfolio.** Create a powerful portfolio by including the 10 things described in Chapter 20 of your textbook. Be sure to organize and display your work and documents in a book or binder you will be proud to show to a potential employer.

Fun Fact...

The Americans with Disabilities Act prohibits general inquiries about health problems, disabilities, and medical conditions during an interview.

Quick Review!

chapter 20: seeking employment review

Complete the multiple-choice questions below by circling the correct answer to each question.

1. What type of question formats will you find in the written state board licensing exam?
   a. Essay
   b. Multiple choice
   c. Matching
   d. All of the above

2. What is the most important strategy of written test taking?
   a. Knowing your material
   b. Skipping answers you don't know
   c. Watching for key words or terms
   d. Eliminating options you know to be incorrect

3. Which of the following are strategies associated with deductive reasoning?
   a. Eliminate options know to be incorrect
   b. Watch for key words or terms
   c. Look for similar or related questions that may provide answers
   d. All of the above

4. What type of questions should you ask if you have the opportunity to network with industry professionals?
   a. How much money they make
   b. What they like most and least about their current positions
   c. Tips that will assist you in your search for the right establishment
   d. B and C

5. Which of the following will yield the best information about possible employment when you begin your job search?
   a. Placement assistance program
   b. Postings on the school bulletin boards
   c. Phone book
   d. A and B

6. Which of the following will most help you to get the position you want and keep it?
   a. Good looks
   b. Good technical and communication skills
   c. Strong work ethic
   d. B and C

7. A written summary of your education and work experience is called:
   a. A biography
   b. An essay
   c. A resume
   d. None of the above

8. What is the average time spent reading a resume before the owner or manager decides whether to grant you an interview?

    a. 20 seconds

    b. 1 minute

    c. 5 minutes

    d. However long it takes to read the resume

9. Which of the following describes the best rationale for writing your resume?

    a. To explain all the jobs and skills you have had in your life

    b. To market yourself so the reader will want to meet you

    c. To make yourself look as important as possible

    d. A and B

10. What should you not put on your resume?

    a. Education history

    b. Personal references

    c. Salary history

    d. B and C

11. Which of the following forms of identification should you take to an interview?

    a. Marriage license and birth certificate

    b. Names, addresses, and phone numbers of former employers

    c. Name and phone number of the nearest relative not living with you

    d. B and C

12. When should you start looking for your first salon position?

    a. Before you graduate from school

    b. As soon as you graduate from school

    c. After you take your state board exam

    d. After you receive your license or permit

13. When interviewing, which communications should be in writing?

    a. Confirmation of your meeting time and date

    b. A thank-you note after your visit

    c. Initial contact letter

    d. A and B

14. Which of the following should you have with you when on an interview?

    a. Social Security card and driver's license

    b. Resume, cover letter, and employment portfolio

    c. References

    d. All of the above

15. Which of the following question(s) are illegal for an employer to ask during an interview?

    a. How old are you?

    b. Are you authorized to work in the United States?

    c. Which languages are you fluent in?

    d. A and B

what would you do? a salon **scenario**

You have a date with your friend to go to the movies tonight, but you just received a phone call from Top to Toe nail salon, and the owner of the salon would like to meet with you tomorrow morning at 9:00am for an interview. She has already read your resume and cover letter, and would like to see a sample of your work. She also asked that you perform a manicure during your interview if possible. What will you do to get prepared tonight?

_____

_____

_____

_____

_____

_____

_____

_____

_____

_____

_____

_____

_____

_____

21 on the job

Congratulations! You have studied hard in nail school and will soon be taking your licensing exam—you are now launching your career as a nail technician! Okay, you can breathe a quick sigh of relief and you take a few minutes to revel in your excitement, but don't forget all that you have learned about prioritizing your goals and committing to personal rules of conduct and behavior.

Guess why—the goals and rules learned in chapter 21 will help guide you throughout your career!

salon terms double puzzle

Write the answers in the cells, using the clues provided. Copy the letters in the numbered cells to the other cells with the same number to reveal the secret message!

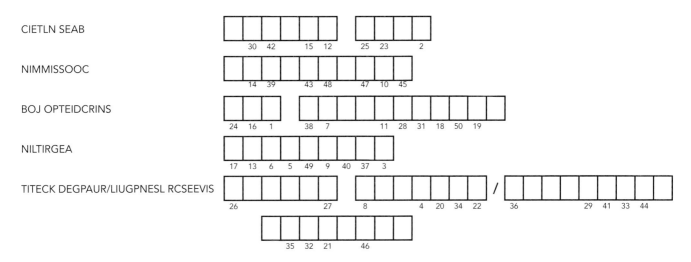

CIETLN SEAB

NIMMISSOOC

BOJ OPTEIDCRINS

NILTIRGEA

TITECK DEGPAUR/LIUGPNESL RCSEEVIS

Clues

1. Customers who are loyal to a particular nail technician.
2. Percentage of revenue that a salon takes in from sales earmarked for the practitioner.
3. Document that outlines the duties and responsibilities of a particular position.
4. Act of recommending and selling quality products to clients for at-home nail care.
5. Practice of recommending and selling additional services to clients that may be performed by you or other practitioners licensed in a different field.

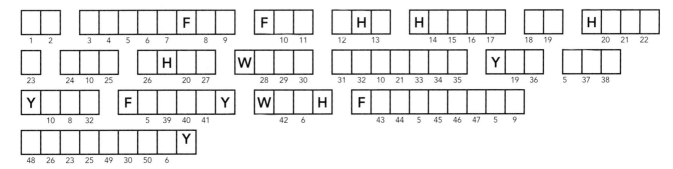

Working in a Salon

understanding clients and co-workers

When working in the nail industry there are things you must do and remember in order to be successful. You will most likely be working with others in the salon and therefore must learn how to be part of a team, while your world revolves around serving your clients. Using the information you learned in chapter 21, answer True or False to the statements below that will help guide you towards perfecting your people skills.

T   F   **1.** Put your own feelings or desires aside and put the needs of the business and the client first.

T   F   **2.** Be true to your word. Do what you say you will do.

T   F   **3.** Be punctual. Scheduling is central to the nail business.

T   F   **4.** If you become unhappy and start acting out in an ungrateful, disrespectful manner, it may be time to consider changing salons.

T   F   **5.** Be respectful, even if you may not like or agree with someone.

T   F   **6.** A valued nail professional is one who intends to keep on learning.

T   F   **7.** Do your own job; try to refrain from performing other duties as it might offend others.

T   F   **8.** Use every situation to provide yourself an opportunity to take your career to the next level.

T   F   **9.** Find ways to resolve problems constructively and quickly.

T   F   **10.** Gain more insight into your own behavior, how to better deal with people, and how to improve your business skills.

T   F   **11.** Stay a little later, or come in a little earlier, to help out a teammate.

T   F   **12.** Don't share what you know, this will make you seem conceited to others.

T   F   **13.** Given the stress of a typical salon, you should limit your work hours.

T   F   **14.** Resist all temptations to become negative or give in to gossip.

T   F   **15.** Never work toward resolving conflict, staying out of it is a safe move.

compensation mini quiz

Compensation varies from one salon to another. In the space provided, explain the different income opportunities and types of payment you can expect to earn as a nail technician.

1. Hourly Salary

_____

_____

_____

_____

_____

2. Weekly Salary

_____

_____

_____

3. Commission

_____

_____

_____

_____

_____

4. Hourly Salary Plus Commissions

_____

_____

_____

_____

_____

5. Tips

_____

_____

_____

_____

_____

6. Ticket upgrading, or upselling services

_____

_____

_____

7. Retailing

_____

_____

_____

_____

Fun **Fact...**

The standard retail sales commission for a nail technician is 10 percent of her/his total retail sales per week. Couple that with upselling services and you can easily make hundreds of dollars more per month.

practice retailing!

Select a nail product and a partner from class and role-play the dynamics of a sales situation. Take turns being the customer and the nail technician. Evaluate each other on how you did, with suggestions about where you can improve. Then try this exercise with someone else, so you can get different points of view on how well you do. Remember: no two customers are the same!

Managing Your Money
your personal budget

In addition to making money, responsible adults are also concerned with meeting their financial responsibilities, paying back their debts, and planning for the future. Go through the budget worksheet below and fill in the amounts that apply to your current living and financial situation. If you are unsure of the amount of an expense, put in the amount you have averaged over the past three months or give it your best guess. For your income, you may need to have three or four months of employment history to answer, but fill in what you can. Then answer the questions on the following page to evaluate your current financial situation.

Personal Budget Worksheet

A. Expenses

1. My monthly rent (or share of the rent) is $_____
2. My monthly car payment is   _____
3. My monthly car insurance payment is   _____
4. My monthly auto fuel/upkeep expenses are   _____
5. My monthly electric bill is   _____
6. My monthly gas bill is   _____
7. My monthly health insurance payment is   _____
8. My monthly entertainment expense is   _____
9. My monthly bank fees are   _____
10. My monthly grocery expense is   _____
11. My monthly dry cleaning expense is   _____
12. My monthly personal grooming expense is   _____
13. My monthly prescription/medical expense is   _____
14. My monthly telephone is   _____
15. My monthly student loan payment is   _____
16. My IRA payment is   _____
17. My savings account deposit is   _____
18. Other expenses: _____

TOTAL EXPENSES $_____

B. Income

1. My monthly take-home pay is   _____
2. My monthly income from tips is   _____
3. Other income: _____

TOTAL INCOME $_____

C. Balance

Total Income (B)   _____
Minus Total Expenses (A)   _____

BALANCE $_____

---

1. How do your expenses compare to your income?

_____

_____

_____

_____

2. What is your balance after all your expenses are paid?

_____

_____

_____

_____

3. Were you surprised by any of the information in this exercise? Explain.

_____

_____

_____

_____

4. Why is keeping a budget a good way to manage your money?

_____

_____

_____

_____

5. Do you know any other methods people use to manage money that could be helpful to you?

_____

_____

_____

_____

How To Expand Your Client Base

marketing puzzle

Great and fun marketing can really help you to expand your client base. Below are some ideas for ways to market yourself, fill in the missing words in each statement and then find your answers in the word find puzzle on the following page.

1. Ask clients for their _____ on the client consultation card, and then one month before, send a card with a _____.

2. Don't _____ clients by _____ through your services. Providing good-quality, _____ services must always be your first concern.

3. Always be _____, _____, _____, and _____. Be at the salon when you say you will be there, and give your clients the nail length and shape they ask for.

4. Recommend a ____ _____ only when you have tried it yourself and you know what it can and cannot do.

5. When you treat others with _____, you become worthy of it yourself. This means that you do not _____ or _____ of anyone or anything. _____ energy brings everyone _____, especially you.

6. Look for the _____ in every situation. No one enjoys being around a person who is always __ _____.

7. Be _____; it is your job to be the client's _____, not their psychiatrist or a _____.

8. Give clients _____ to recommend you to others. Give your client your _____ with her name on the back. Ask her to hand these out to her friends and associates and for every one you get back, give her a _____ on her next service.

9. To build a feeling of _____ among local vendors and to reach new clients, offer to have a _____ and commit to _____ your clients to them when they are in the market for goods or services that your neighbors can provide, if they will do the same for you.

10. Put together a _____ where you might _____ professional appearance and nail grooming tips for local women's groups, such as the PTA, or organizations for young men and women, or anywhere that will put you in front of people in your community, who are all _____.

```
Y R P R K T P N G D S I P L C N R L R J
M U O Y E M H G W J S S W A O A E A S C
C O X L F F N O R O Y S U U U I T N T S
T A T D E F F E U C D D N T R L A O N T
E Y B I M S S O H G F I S C T T I I E I
D M P D V P N I L T H S O N E E L S I W
B R J O E A A U N A G T B U O C P S L S
I X A C M T T E O Z I P F P U H R E C H
R H T C R R T I Q C B C M U S N O F L O
T Y V I S S B I O P E A E P L I D O A R
H W S G I S F D B N K G A P L C U R I T
D T B S Y G E M I E J W A P S I C P T P
A K N N T N T N F S S E O I R A T Z N R
Y O R E I I G U I D C S S E R N Q Y E O
C J U G N R N E R S I O L O T R P H T G
N U S A U R Z A V T U I U L L P A S O R
L W H T M E C E I I A B J N A V D M P A
X I I I M F E V Y B I B O H T H X S P M
I H N V O E E L L E G D N S S U C S I D
E O G E C R Q E W X Z U G O S S I P X P
```

chapter 21: on the job review

Complete the multiple-choice questions below by circling the correct answer to each question.

1. What two opportunities will you have to increase your income in a salon besides asking for a raise?
   a. Retailing
   b. Ticket upgrading
   c. Assisting others
   d. A and B

2. The first thing to remember when you are in a service business is:
   a. It will take many hours of practice to become great
   b. There will be a lot of slow/down time
   c. Your work revolves around serving your clients
   d. It will take a long time to build a clientele

3. Nail technicians can increase their chances of building a solid and loyal clientele more quickly if they:
   a. Have advanced training, skills, and certifications
   b. Employ marketing and publicity strategies
   c. Concentrate on an unusual niche within the nail business
   d. All of the above

4. Creating a _____ will ensure that you and your employer have a good understanding of what is expected of you.
   a. Employment portfolio
   b. Job description
   c. Resume
   d. All of the above

5. Most nail technicians must research and plan for _____ on their own.
   a. Health and dental insurance
   b. Retirement accounts
   c. Savings accounts
   d. All of the above

6. The best way to meet all of your financial responsibilities is to know:
   a. What you owe and what you earn
   b. What you need and what you will have
   c. What you want and what is possible
   d. What you have and what you want

7. How can you generate a greater income for yourself, without asking your employer for a raise or asking for a higher percentage of commission?
    a. Spend less money
    b. Increase your service prices
    c. Work longer hours
    d. A and B

8. A _____ raise per service is a great way to increase your income each week, without it costing clients so much that they consider not using your services any longer.
    a. $1.00
    b. $2.00
    c. $3.00
    d. $4.00

9. To be successful in sales, you need:
    a. Ambition
    b. Determination
    c. A good personality
    d. All of the above

10. The foundation for successful selling is recognizing the client's:
    a. Abilities
    b. Needs
    c. Preferences
    d. B and C

11. What do you need to successfully sell retail products to nail clients?
    a. An incentive program that rewards everyone—the salon, the nail tech, and the client!
    b. A positive attitude—no one wants to buy products from a person who is not genuinely happy to be at the salon.
    c. Smart promotional pricing and/or some kind of added value for the client who is making the purchase.
    d. All of the above.

12. How do you get the conversation started about retailing products?
    a. Place products in the clients' hands, or have them in view
    b. Advise clients about how recommended services will benefit them
    c. Inform clients about any promotions and sales that are going on
    d. All of the above

13. Rebooking clients before they leave the salon will ensure:
    a. They receive the care they need, when they need it
    b. Your client will show up for her next appointment
    c. Your appointment book remains filled
    d. A and C

14. The best way to encourage your client to book another appointment before she leaves is to:

   a. Ask questions during the service and listen carefully to her answers

   b. Offer her a discount on her next service

   c. Take her to the receptionist and have her ask for the next appointment

   d. None of the above

15. While you are working on a client's nails, you can begin the conversation of her next appointment by talking about:

   a. The condition of their nails

   b. What her schedule is like in the upcoming weeks

   c. Benefits of regular maintenance services

   d. A and C

what would you do? a salon **scenario**

You have a family vacation planned in four weeks and you would like to increase your income by $200 per week for the next four weeks to have some extra spending money on your trip! You are a weekly booth renter in a full service salon, so after your booth rent is paid, you keep the rest of your income. You receive 20 percent commission on any retail products you sell.

You won't be able to work any more than your standard five days, but you can stay an extra hour every day you are working. What would you do to increase your profits for the next four weeks? Create a marketing plan and budget to show how you can earn this $800 additional income.

_____

_____

_____

_____

_____

_____

_____

_____

22

the salon
business

As you become more proficient in your craft and your ability to manage yourself and others, you may decide to become an independent booth renter, or even a salon owner. While this may seem like an easy thing to do, being a successful business person requires experience, a genuine love of people, and solid business management skills.

In this chapter we will review the general overview of the salon business and what it will take to open your own business.

Key Terms

salon business terms

Fill in the crossword puzzle with key words found in chapter 22, by using the clues below.

ACROSS

2 Business structure in which two or more- people share ownership, although not necessarily equally; management and responsibilities of the business and its operations may be given to one or more people.

3 Supplies used in daily business operations.

5 The one and only owner and manager of a business.

6 Employees, staff.

8 Supplies sold to clients.

9 Written plan of a business, as it is seen in the present and envisioned in the future.

10 A long-term picture of what the business is to become and what it will look like when it gets there.

11 Renting a booth or station in a salon; also known as a chair rental.

DOWN

1 A description of the key strategic influences of the business, such as the market it will serve, the kinds of services it will offer, and the quality of those services.

3 Money needed to start a business.

4 Business whose ownership is shared by three or more people called stockholders.

7 A set of benchmarks that, once achieved, help you to realize your mission and your vision.

Going Into Business For Yourself

booth rental vs. salon ownersthip

Many people see booth rental as a more desirable alternative to owning a salon. Read the statements below and circle True or False according to what you've learned about booth renting and salon ownership in chapter 22.

A booth renter:

T　F　**1.** Rents a station or workspace in a salon from the salon owner.

T　F　**2.** Is only provided furniture, telephone, towels, insurance, laundry, and record-keeping by the salon, the rest is up to the booth renter.

T　F　**3.** Uses the salon's telephone and booking system.

T　F　**4.** Depends on the salon to collect all service fees, whether they are paid by cash or credit card

T　F　**5.** Pays the salon owner a flat fee for use of the booth on a daily, weekly, biweekly, or monthly basis.

T　F　**6.** Keeps the same hours of operation as the salon.

T　F　**7.** Maintains expenses that are fairly low.

T　F　**8.** Benefits if she/he has a large, steady clientele and does not have to rely on the salon to keep busy.

T　F　**9.** Does not have to keep records for income tax purposes and other legal reasons, the way a salon owner has to.

T　F　**10.** Purchases all supplies, including back-bar and retail, and maintains her/his own inventory.

T　F　**11.** Does not have to budget for advertising, as the salon provides that for them.

T　F　**12.** Pays all taxes, including higher Social Security, double that of an employee.

T　F　**13.** Is automatically covered under the salon's malpractice insurance and health insurance plans.

T　F　**14.** Has all professional salon materials, including business cards and service menus provided for her/him.

T　F　**15.** Pays for all of her/his own continuing education.

Salon owners:

T　F　**16.** Must create a long-term picture of what the business is to become and what it will look like when it gets there.

T　F　**17.** Should base the business's location in an area that is convenient to the primary clientele and their needs.

PROFIT

LOSS

© IMAGERYMAJESTIC, 2010. USED UNDER LICENSE FROM SHUTTERSTOCK.COM

T F **18.** Can name the business anything she/he desires, as the name will not influence how clients and potential clients perceive the business.

T F **19.** Must purchase and carry adequate business insurance.

T F **20.** Must be aware of OSHA guidelines and how to comply with them.

T F **21.** Could take a year or more to determine and complete all of the aspects of starting the business.

T F **22.** Should only take two years tending to the business, its clientele and employees for the business to be profitable.

T F **23.** Should wait only two to five years before adding additional locations, expanding the scope of the business (adding spa services around current services), or constructing a larger space, or anything else clients may need.

T F **24.** Should be able to read, interpret, and generate business records.

T F **25.** Must be versed in business regulations and laws.

Fun **Fact...**

Small businesses represent more than 99 percent of all employers and provide 60 percent to 80 percent of new jobs annually.

Source: http://www.smbtn.com/smallbusinessfacts

business plan double puzzle

Regardless of the type of salon you plan to own, it is imperative to have a thorough and well-researched business plan to follow throughout the entire process of starting your own business. Identify the kind of information and material that should be included in a business plan by using the clues below. Write your answer inside the cells, and then copy the letters in the numbered cells to the cells with the same number to reveal the secret message!

NAOSL SIPCOILE

XEUVICEET MUYMASR

NIGMEKTAR NAPL

LANAFNICI COMDUESNT

SINSIOM TESTENMAT

NIANALZOGTORAI PALN

OSVINI TANESETTM

GOUPIPRNTS TMSEUDONC

Clues

1. Even small salons and booth renters should have policies that they adhere to. These ensure that all clients and employees are treated fairly and consistently.
2. Summarizes your plan and states your objectives.
3. Outlines all of the research obtained regarding the clients your business will target and their needs, wants, and habits.
4. Includes the projected financial statements, actual (historical) statements, and financial statement analysis.
5. A description of the key strategic influences of the business, such as the market it will serve, the kinds of services it will offer, and the quality of those services.
6. Outlines employees and management levels and also describes how the business will run administratively.
7. A long-term picture of what the business is to become and what it will look like when it gets there.
8. Includes owners resume, personal financial information, legal contracts, and any other agreements, etc.

Secret Message:

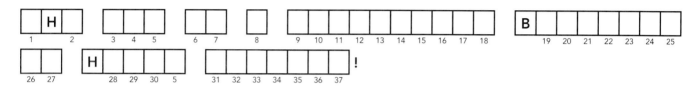

| H | | | | | | | | | | | | | | | | | | | | | B | | | | | | |
| 1 | | 2 | 3 | 4 | 5 | | 6 | 7 | | 8 | | 9 | 10 | 11 | 12 | 13 | 14 | 15 | 16 | 17 | 18 | | 19 | 20 | 21 | 22 | 23 | 24 | 25 |

| | | H | | | | | | | | | | | ! |
| 26 | 27 | | 28 | 29 | 30 | 5 | | 31 | 32 | 33 | 34 | 35 | 36 | 37 |

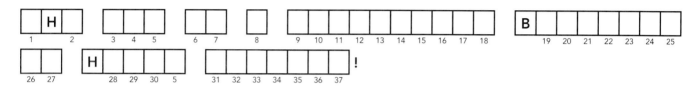

Fun **Fact...**

Girl power! Women own 10.4 million businesses in the United States (nearly 50 percent or more), generating $1.9 trillion in sales. For the past two decades, majority women-owned firms have continued to grow at around two times the rate of all firms.

Source: http://www.smbtn.com/smallbusinessfacts

Operating A Successful Salon

main elements mini quiz

There are five important elements to keep in mind when planning to open a salon. Use the space below to describe the most important factors in each of these main elements of planning and operating a successful salon business.

1. Salon Layout

_____

_____

_____

_____

_____

_____

_____

_____

2. Personnel

_____

_____

_____

_____

_____

_____

_____

_____

_____

3. The Front Desk

_____

_____

_____

_____

_____

_____

_____

_____

_____

4. Efficiently Using Telephones

_____

_____

_____

_____

_____

_____

_____

_____

_____

5. Advertising salon services

_____

_____

_____

_____

_____

_____

_____

_____

draw this!

On the blank billboard below draw a colorful advertisement for your personally owned salon using only one word to describe it!

chapter 22: the salon business review

Complete the multiple-choice questions below by circling the correct answer to each question.

1. As a nail technician, in what ways can you go into business for yourself?
   a. Managing a salon
   b. Independent booth renter
   c. Salon owner
   d. B and C

2. When preparing a business plan, a _____ can be invaluable in helping you gather accurate financial information.
   a. Certified public accountant or CPA
   b. Seasoned nail technician
   c. Another small business owner
   d. All of the above

3. How can a salon business be owned and operated?
   a. Sole proprietorship
   b. Partnership
   c. Stockholder of a corporation
   d. All of the above

4. If you are not the only owner, your lease must clearly specify:
   a. Who owns what
   b. How long you plan to be in business together
   c. Who is responsible for which repairs and expenses
   d. A and C

5. A simple and efficient _____ system is necessary to have a good business operation.
   a. Payroll
   b. Banking
   c. Record-keeping
   d. A and B

6. Record-keeping includes keeping track of salon inventory. What does an inventory system cover?
   a. Purchase records
   b. Inventory on shelves
   c. Identifies theft or shrinkage
   d. All of the above

7. When designing a new salon, _____ should be your top consideration.
   a. Maximum efficiency
   b. Clean, modern decor
   c. Plumbing
   d. A and C

8. What is the one thing you must do to guarantee that you will stay in business and have a prosperous salon?
   a. Make sure your staff is happy
   b. Take excellent care of your clients
   c. Create a beautiful, clean, functional salon
   d. Keep all your finances and bookkeeping in order

9. What should you consider when interviewing a potential employee?
   a. Level of technical and communication skills
   b. Personal grooming and attitude
   c. Age and personal habits
   d. A and B

10. In terms of finances, your top priority is to:
    a. Make the mortgage or rental payment
    b. Be sure to have enough funds for supplies and retail
    c. Make your payroll without fail
    d. Ensure you can re-pay your business loan payment

11. What part of your salon should make a strong first impression?
    a. Pedicure room
    b. Manicure tables
    c. Parking lot
    d. Reception area

12. What information must be included for every salon appointment?
    a. Name
    b. Contact information
    c. Specific services
    d. All of the above

13. What is the best form of advertising?
    a. Business cards
    b. A satisfied client
    c. Commercial
    d. Coupon in a local paper

14. An important aspect of the salon's financial success revolves around the sale of:
    a. Gift certificates
    b. Salon services
    c. Home maintenance products
    d. B and C

15. As a beauty industry professional, you are making customer care your top priority so when retailing products and services, your customers will feel:
    a. You are being pushy
    b. You are trying to get more money out of them
    c. You are offering them good advice
    d. You are trying to brag about how much you know

Part5

PREPARING FOR THE PRACTICAL EXAM
BONUS CHAPTERS

23

before you graduate

Okay...you've taken all of the quizzes, read all of the chapters, practiced all of the procedures and now you really are ready to go out there, get licensed and get your work life underway!

Don't fret; we are going to get you ready for the next steps in the following workbook chapters. The previous workbook chapters aligned perfectly with your textbook and used games and puzzles to help you to learn, review and remember the principles and data in your text that will assist you when taking the written exam. This section is going to give you all of the info—including checklists—that will guide you through preparing for and taking your practical, or hands-on part of your exam.

This is important stuff...so put on your thinking cap and let's get started!

Necessary Information

Let's begin with some very important information—what you need to know about your state's exam requirements!

In this section, you will need to do the research necessary to ensure you know the proper procedures and regulations for **your** state's licensing exam. So, as you fill in the blanks for your state requirements throughout this section, you **must** research the most up-to-date information. You can get accurate info by:

1. Speaking to your instructors.

2. Going online to your state's licensing website.

3. Calling your state's licensing division.

Okay, let's get rolling…

 ## my state licensing division information:

My state: _____

Name of Division: _____

Address:_____

Phone Number: _____

Website: _____

Email Contact: _____

The Licensing Exam

Some states administer a national nail examination while other states administer a state-designed nail examination. In either case, the exam consists of two parts, a written and practical exam. In some states you will have to complete the written exam before you can apply to take the practical exam. Ordinarily you will be scheduled to take both in the same day. The procedures to be performed during the practical exam will vary from state to state, but all will consider health and safety a primary concern and the procedures will have an allotted completion time. To get an idea of your state's required procedures and time allotments, you can ask your instructor or call your licensing division.

 my state's requirement:

Check the areas you will be required to demonstrate during your practical nail exam:

- ☐ table setup
- ☐ table setup including basic manicure setup
- ☐ basic manicure on one hand
- ☐ monomer liquid and polymer powder nail enhancement (one nail)
- ☐ nail tip application (one nail)
- ☐ nail wrap enhancement (one nail)
- ☐ polish application (one hand)
- ☐ hand massage (one hand)
- ☐ arm massage (one arm)
- ☐ nail art/flat art
- ☐ repair techniques
- ☐ Other: _____

procedure time allotment

The following time allotments have been provided as a general idea of what is allowed. You will need to find out your states actual requirements.

 my state's requirement:

Actual	General	
_____	20 min	Initial table setup including setting up for a basic manicure
_____	20 min	Basic manicure (one hand)
_____	20 min	Polish application (all nails on manicured hand)
_____	20 min	Nail tip application (one finger)
_____	20 min	Nail wrap enhancement (one finger)
_____	20 min	Monomer liquid and polymer powder enhancement (one finger)

_____	20 min	Flat nail art (if required)
_____	15 min	Final cleanup

your exam date

You will apply for an exam date when you have completed your required hours and testing in school. There will be a form you will fill out to apply for your licensing exam, and this form will need to be sent to the licensing division along with your school records and possibly an exam fee. Once you have been scheduled to take the licensing exam you will be sent an examination or admission notice. This notice will give you the location, date, and time for the exam, along with the required procedures you will perform during the practical examination. It may also list rules and regulations about the practical exam, identification or documentation needed to enter the exam room, as well as specific products needed or allowed. You will need to review this information carefully so that you understand everything that is required of you. You may want to make a photocopy so that you can make notes in the margins or highlight areas of importance.

necessary documentation for your examination admittance

State licensing examinations require you to present specific documentation in order to be admitted into the examination site. If you do not present the required documentation you may not be allowed to take the test! So, make sure you know what identification is expected and make sure you have it with you, as the requirements will vary from state to state.

Many states require you to have an official picture identification card; if you don't have one (driver's license with photo for example), you may be allowed to present a personal picture that is notarized and has your signature. See your instructor or trainer for more information concerning this area.

my state's requirements:

☐ official picture identification

☐ Social Security card

☐ model's official identification

☐ fee payment of $ _____

Tech Tip:

Some states require you to pay the exam fee upon admittance into the exam site, others require you prepay the fee when you apply for your examination. Failure to show up for your examination may cause you to forfeit your fee if you've paid in advance, and you will be required to pay the fee again before being rescheduled for another examination.

Your Personal Appearance At The Exam

The old saying "when you look good, you feel good" has high merit. You actually perform better when your physical appearance meets the circumstances of the occasion.

clothing and accessories

During exams, states customarily require that your clothing and kits be free from personal names, school names, salon names, or logos. This allows the examiners to evaluate you in a completely objective manner, and also prevents any judgment by the participants that they are being discriminated against or favored for any reason.

Your state board may require you to wear specific clothing, such as a uniform, closed-toe shoes, a protective outer covering, or other designated articles of clothing. If no specific clothing is required, ask your instructor or trainer for suggestions or direction. Regardless, your clothing should look good, radiating your professionalism, knowledge, and confidence in your skills.

You will also want to limit the amount of jewelry you wear on test day. It's better to be safe than sorry...so why not leave your earrings, necklaces, and rings at home? And, for safe measure, ask your model to do the same. If you wear jewelry to the exam, it should not dangle or make noise in any way, nor should it be so obtrusive that it gets in your way!

Your appearance will convey one of two messages: "I am capable of caring for myself, and therefore I am capable of caring for others' appearance," or, "I can't take care of myself, so how am I going to take care of others?" You have only one chance to make a good impression. This is a very important time to make not only a good impression, but also a great impression.

hair and nails

Your hair should be clean and styled to enhance your professional appearance, and concentrated care should be given to your nails to ensure a professional appearance, especially during a nail-based exam. Your hands should be spotlessly clean; your nails should be well-manicured and they should be at a length to allow you to easily execute the procedure manipulations required during your exam. Even though you are trained in the nail care area, excessive nail art and nail jewelry should be avoided because it is not considered professional for a state practical nail exam, and it is very distracting.

posture

During your nail exam you will be sitting. Therefore, the examiners will observe your sitting posture. Remember to always sit up straight and look alert and confident.

You should sit with your lower back against the chair, learning slightly forward. Keep your feet and knees close together, and keep your feet flat on the floor. Keep your shoulders straight to avoid a slouched appearance. If you are required to sit on a stool, sit on the complete stool, not on the edges. Displaying "professional" posture will assure the examiners that you are well-trained and confident in your skills.

attitude

It is important to project a professional, positive attitude and self-confidence during your practical examination. These traits are detectable and can be observed by the examiners during your examination.

Trust yourself and your knowledge, never allow another participant to influence your training or thoughts. Keep your mind and eyes on your own work. You know what you were taught in your school or salon and what you have practiced and mastered. If you forget a procedure, relax, take a deep, relaxing breath and take a moment to refresh your memory. Don't wait to see what someone else is doing.

Never change the way you perform a procedure. If another participant is performing a procedure differently than you, do not let this influence you. Do not change or modify what you were taught and practiced. If you were taught to apply a monomer liquid and polymer powder nail or a nail tip or another procedure in a specific manner, chances are you were taught properly. You have no idea what other participants learned or where they trained, but you do know what you were taught and learned.

Model Or Mannequin

 my state's requirements:

Check which you will be required to use during your practical exam:

☐ Model

☐ Plastic mannequin hand

Note: All procedures in PART 5 of your textbook will reference the use of a live model. However, if you are required to use a mannequin hand instead of a live model, the mannequin hand should be treated as if you were performing the services or demonstrations on a live model including using all health and safety procedures on the mannequin.

choosing a model

If you are required to bring a model to your practical examination, you should start the selection process four to six weeks before graduation. State testing agencies designate specific requirements for models, such as their age, and that they must not be a past or present student in a nail technology or cosmetology school, or not be licensed in any area in the field of nail care or cosmetology.

Select a model that will be able to attend your examination on the day you are scheduled to take your practical examination. Most states do not permit your model to have any type of nail enhancements on her natural nails during your examination, so it's best to choose a model that has great natural nails!

You should be sure your model is flexible in allowing you to perform the required procedures and inform her in advance of the procedures you will be performing. You should also practice your procedures every week with your model's nails to familiarize yourself with them.

the model's nails

The model's nails must be a specified length in order for you to adequately demonstrate your procedures. Most states require that the nails have at least 1/8 of an inch free edge. It is common for the state to require the model have no enhancement products on any of her nails at the start of the examination, so you will want to be sure to choose a model with beautiful, strong natural nails. Some states require that your model's nail(s) be polished prior to your admission into the practical exam. You will remove the polish at the beginning of the manicure procedure as part of the exam.

You will want to ensure that you see your model the day before your licensing exam to prepare her nails exactly as required for the examination. Be sure to follow your state licensing directions for the requirements and preparation of your model's nails located on your examination notice. Until you receive your notice you may check with your instructor for your state's specific model requirements and the specific guidelines for your model's preparation.

my state's requirements:

Model guidelines: _____

_____

_____

Model nail preparation guidelines: _____

_____

_____

model checklist

- [ ] Select a dependable model 4-6 weeks before graduation that fits your specific state requirements.

- [ ] Make sure you have explained to your model the procedures you will be required to perform during the practical examination.

- [ ] Make sure your model has the required official documentation for entrance into the examination.

- [ ] Make sure that your model's nails are adequate in length and in good condition (most states require at least 1/8 of an inch free nail edge).

- [ ] Work with your model's nails once a week before the examination.

- [ ] Complete any mandatory preparation on your model's nails the day before your practical examination and ask her to be careful not to harm or break a nail before she accompanies you on exam day.

- [ ] Have your model sign the model commitment form.

model commitment form

It can be helpful to use a form such as the one below to ensure your model understands her commitment, and the importance of her participation and cooperation in your practical exam preparation and the actual exam day.

I, _____, have agreed to be a model for the
(Model's Name)

practical examination of _____.
(Student's Name)

I understand that I will be contacted as soon as the examination date is scheduled and that I will make arrangements in my schedule to attend.

I verify that I am at least 18 years of age and have an acceptable form of official picture identification.

I also acknowledge that I am not presently, nor have I been in the past, licensed in any field within the cosmetology/nail industry, and that I am not presently a student in any cosmetology/nail industry–related school.

I further understand and agree to have the following procedures performed on me during his or her practice and practical examination:

1. _____

2. _____

3. _____

4. _____

5. _____

6. _____

I further agree to make myself available for at least 6-8 practice sessions before the exam date. I understand that these practice sessions will range from 1-3 hours and end in a manicure.

I agree to inform _____ immediately if any
(Student's Name)
unforeseen circumstances should occur that would prevent or alter any agreed upon commitments by me in this form.

Signed: _____ Date: _____
(Model's Signature)

Signed: _____ Date: _____
(Student's Signature)

using a mannequin hand at your state examination

If you are required to use a mannequin hand during your practical exam make sure that the fingers are flexible enough to permit you to perform your procedures adequately and ensure that your mannequin hand fits properly on your hand holder or stand. If the hand does not fit properly it could make it difficult for you to properly perform all of the procedures you need to. You should also check to ensure that your holder/stand will securely and properly attach, to your work area (table).

Your Kit For The State Practical Examination

Consult your instructor, trainer, or admission notice for instructions on specific requirements for your kit's contents and organization. Most states require you to use your kit as a dry sanitizer. So, you will be directed to keep your kit closed except when removing and replacing the supplies, material, and equipment you need for each specific procedure.

Your state may allow you to rent a kit. If this is the case, you are responsible for making sure all of the required supplies, implements, and equipment are present. It is your responsibility to be sure that the contents and condition of your kit are complete and functional. Unfortunately, examiners cannot make concessions if there is a problem of any type due to the condition or contents of a rented kit.

Chapter 23: Points To Remember

☐ Find a reliable source for asking questions about your licensing exam.

☐ Secure a model 4-6 weeks before graduation (if required).

☐ Find out the procedures and time allotments for your state's practical exam.

☐ Locate the form to apply for your licensing exam.

☐ Practice on your model once a week before your exam.

24

packing
for the exam

Preparation for your practical examination requires time and effort. To feel confident, you will want to know what is required of you during the exam and pack everything that you will need. There is nothing worse than showing up unprepared!

Use this chapter to help you identify the tools, equipment and documents you will need for your state board exam and start getting ready well in advance of your exam date!

Your State Practical Examination Kit

You will need to assemble a kit that includes everything you will need for your licensing exam including: documentation, pencils, pens, products, equipment, and supplies needed for your practical examination. Your kit may be carried in a large bag or rolling case depending upon the amount of products and equipment needed for your examination.

Some states will specify the size and the type of kit you are required to bring and use during your state practical exam. Consult your instructor, trainer, or admission notice for instructions about how to set up your kit's contents.

proper documentation

You will not be admitted into the examination room without your required documentation. As soon as you receive your admission notice and other required documentation, place them in your kit. This will allow you to have easy access to them once you arrive at your examination site. You will also want to make a note of any other documents or identification you need to bring to your exam, and attach it to the outside of your kit, so you won't forget to add them to your kit on the day of your exam. These required items will be listed on your admissions notice.

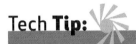

Tech Tip:

If you need the documentation for review during your preparation, make yourself a copy, so the original documentation remains in your kit.

implements and supplies

It is imperative that you have all of the mandated implements and supplies listed on your admission notice to perform the required procedures during your examination. Missing implements and supplies may cause you to be disqualified from performing specific required procedures and possibly even to be disqualified from your examination. It only stands to reason that if you do not have the required implements and supplies for a specific procedure, then you cannot perform it; therefore, you cannot possibly be graded on or pass that section of the exam.

If you pack all the required materials for each procedure in a separate, labeled mini kit, you will be less likely to forget needed items and be prompted to remember all of the important components of a procedure, including all safety and sanitation requirements. Packing in this manner will also allow you to perform a quick check of contents for each procedure before you leave for your examination.

If all of the items cannot be placed in your mini kit because of its size or other reasons, make a note of your needed items and place it on the specific procedures mini kit, or place a reminder note on your kit. Another option is to place the items next to your kit. Examples of oversized items include towels, lamps, spray disinfectant, and disinfectant containers.

General Supplies And Materials Needed

You will receive a notice from your examination provider specifying all of the required implements and supplies you are mandated to have when you arrive at your state practical examination. Pack everything that is listed on the notice, two of each in some cases, even if you do not feel it is necessary.

You never know when you may be asked to perform a procedure using some or all of the items and supplies that were listed.

towels

Some states require that you bring a definite number, designated color, and specified size of towels. In addition to meeting the required specifications, your towels should be in good condition and should not have any stains, frayed edges, or holes.

Towels are too large to be placed in a sealed plastic mini kit so it is your responsibility to remember them. Once you know the requirements for your towels, fold and place them in or next to your kit. Another idea is to place a note on top of your kit listing the items that you need to pack. Once the kit is closed the note will remind you of any unpacked items or supplies you need to carry.

If permitted, disposable manicuring towels can be used in lieu of cotton towels. This will allow the examiners to see you properly dispose of your towels and assure them you will change towels between every client. Be guided by your instructor or trainer in this area.

 my state's requirements:

Required color, size and number of towels? _____

Are disposable manicuring towels permitted during your practical exam? _____

condition of implements

All implements and supplies should be in good working condition and they must be cleaned and disinfected. Do not take any implements to the examination that have not been thoroughly cleaned and disinfected. All implements taken to the exam must be in excellent condition. Your metal implements should have smooth edges and be free from visible rust and debris.

labeling supplies and products

All supplies and products that you carry and use during your practical nail exam must have the original manufacturers' labels. Some states may require that your nail enhancement products be in original sealed containers. The seal around the product containers may need to be present and unbroken. If the product does not have a label such as water or alcohol, a handwritten label may be acceptable.

Product labels: _____

_____

trash bag

Label one of your plastic bags *Trash*. Once you have completed a procedure, place all used, disposable items, such as cotton, abrasive boards, wooden pushers, spatulas, and so on, in this bag. Keep your work area clean throughout your practical examination.

contaminated implements bag

Label one of your plastic bags *Contaminated Implements*. Once you have completed a procedure you should place your used reusable items such as your metal cuticle pusher and cuticle nippers (if required) in this bag.

safety glasses/goggles

Safety is a very important area of your examination. Examiners closely monitor and observe your safety techniques. If safety glasses or goggles (if required by your state) are needed for a procedure such as the application of primer or adhesive, make sure you have and put on your safety glasses/goggles.

gloves

Some of the procedures you will be required to demonstrate may suggest that gloves be worn. You should place a pair of gloves in each mini kit for these specific procedures. This will prompt you to put on the gloves when needed. Gloves should also be within reach and used if you accidentally knick yourself, drawing blood, during any procedure. If this happens, you should execute the exposure incident procedure located in your textbook.

© DMYTRO TKACHUK, 2010. USEC UNDER LICENSE FROM SHUTTERSTOCK.COM

health and safety

Health and safety is critical during nail procedures. Throughout the practical exam, the examiners constantly monitor your health and safety techniques.

You will be required to wash your hands and your model's hands and fingers for the procedures you perform during the exam. If you accidentally nick your model or yourself during any procedure, you will be required to perform the exposure incident procedure, so you should have all of the supplies for it on hand.

Here is a checklist of supplies you will need to pack, to handle an exposure incident.

- ☐ Gloves
- ☐ Cotton
- ☐ Antiseptic
- ☐ Adhesive bandages
- ☐ Bio hazard sticker or a container for contaminated waste
- ☐ EPA-registered hospital disinfectant solution
- ☐ Soap and water

You should have a container of disinfectant and a container of spray disinfectant packed for your exam. Pack your liquid disinfectant in a separate closed plastic mini kit, making sure it is sealed tightly to avoid a leak that could get other supplies in your kit wet. You can pack your spray disinfectant in the same manner.

Remember to use a disinfectant product that is registered by the EPA and recognized by your state. Check with your instructor or trainer regarding this topic.

my state's requirements:

Approved disinfectant: _____

Approved antiseptic: _____

Which are you required to use during your practical nail exam?

- ☐ hand sanitizer
- ☐ antiseptic
- ☐ alcohol gel
- ☐ liquid soap for hand washing
- ☐ other

exam kit general items checklist:

- [ ] clear plastic closeable bags (large enough to hold your supplies for specific procedures)
- [ ] additional closeable plastic bags for *contaminated implements* and *trash*; labeled properly
- [ ] small spray bottle labeled *water*
- [ ] permanent marker for labeling your specific procedure mini kits
- [ ] alcohol gel, antiseptic spray, or hand wipes for cleaning purposes.
- [ ] disinfectant
- [ ] disinfectant spray
- [ ] masking tape for attaching your *trash* and *contaminated implements* mini kits to your work area
- [ ] adjustable lamp and extension cord
- [ ] 2-3 light bulbs
- [ ] safety glasses or goggles
- [ ] 5-10 pair of disposable gloves
- [ ] extra plastic bags
- [ ] terrycloth towels, if required
- [ ] disposable towels
- [ ] paper towels
- [ ] No.2 pencil, black ink pen, blue ink pen
- [ ] small watch or clock to keep time (no alarms)
- [ ] admissions notice
- [ ] identification and other documentation required
- [ ] check or money order if you need to pay your exam fee on location

Tech Tip:

It's nice to bring a lamp for extra light, but sometimes electricity to the exam tables is not provided. You may want to find out if this is the case before you pack.

Exam Procedure Mini Kits

Your supplies should be organized and packed in your kit so you can easily access all required implements, products, and equipment. Your kit or carrying case will most likely be used as a dry sanitizer, so you will only be able to open it during table set up and ending clean up.

You will be required to perform specific procedures during your practical exam. If you have the products and tools for each procedure packed separately, they will be easy to locate and you will feel confident that you have everything you need on your table when it's time to start. Pay close attention to each of these sections while you pack your products and tools for your exam to ensure you have everything you need. Remember, you won't be able to borrow anything! If you don't have the right tools and products, you will not be able to perform the procedure.

You will want to be sure to pack **all** the supplies listed on your exam notice. The lists on the following pages contain some items that may *not* be listed on your notice, but may be helpful during your practical nail exam. The supplies lists are separated into mini kits so that you are prompted to complete the proper procedures while setting up your products. This will help keep you organized and on track while setting up your table.

Tech **Tip:**

> Purchase small containers of the required nail products when possible. You will only be demonstrating each procedure on one hand or one finger. Purchasing small bottles of polish remover, cuticle oil, nail polish, lotions, antibacterial soap, and so on saves room and allows you to pack your items in individually-labeled plastic mini kits.

initial table set up and manicure exam

There is a possibility that the examiner will want to grade your table cleanliness before allowing you to set up for your manicure. Pay close attention to the directions given to you, and only complete the table set-up as you are instructed.

You may want to consult your instructor or trainer for specific instructions for setting up your manicure table during your state licensing examination.

Tech **Tip:**

> The table setup outlined here is designed for right-handed nail technicians. If you are left-handed, place the item on the opposite side of the table.

mini kit #1: table cleanliness

- ☐ hand sanitizer/antiseptic
- ☐ approved Environmental Protection Agency (EPA)-registered disinfectant spray
- ☐ paper towels
- ☐ plastic resealable bag labeled *trash*
- ☐ plastic resealable bag labeled *contaminated implements*
- ☐ masking tape (to tape your trash and contaminated implement bags to the side of your manicuring table)

opening mini kit #1 should prompt you to:

1. Clean/wash your hands.

2. Spray your table with disinfectant.

3. Spray your chair/stool and your client's chair/stool with disinfectant.

4. Allow the disinfectant to remain on your table and chair/stool while you tape your *trash* and *contaminated implements* bags to the right side of your table.

5. Wipe your table and chairs/stools with paper towels and place the used paper towels in your *trash* bag.

Tech **Tip:**

Do not perform any other steps until or unless you are directed to do so by your examiner. Once instructed, you should proceed to open mini kits 2 through 7 for your basic manicure table setup.

mini kit #2: implement disinfectant

- ☐ approved EPA-registered liquid disinfectant
- ☐ disinfectant container (wet sanitizer)

Opening mini kit #2 should prompt you to:

1. Pour your liquid, EPA- registered, manufactured labeled, disinfectant into your disinfectant container.

mini kit #3: implements

Pack all required metal implements described on your exam notice in this mini kit.

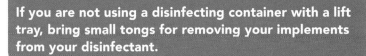

- ☐ metal pusher
- ☐ small scissors
- ☐ nail cutters (for cutting nail tip) or tip cutters
- ☐ cuticle nippers (if allowed and/or required)
- ☐ tweezers or small tongs
- ☐ nail trimmer/clipper

Tech **Tip:**

If you are not using a disinfecting container with a lift tray, bring small tongs for removing your implements from your disinfectant.

Opening mini kit #3 should prompt you to:

1. Place all metal implements from this mini kit into your disinfectant container.

2. Place your specially designated tongs over the edge of your disinfectant container, if needed.

3. Place the cover on your disinfectant container.

mini kit #4: towels

- ☐ clean, laundered, cotton towels
- ☐ disposable paper towels used exclusively for manicuring

Opening mini kit #4 should prompt you to:

1. Place a clean, laundered towel across your table.

2. Place a clean, laundered towel around the hand and arm cushion.

3. Place a disposable manicuring towel in your model's chair/stool.

Tech **Tip:**

If you are unsure of your state's requirement for towels, play it safe. Bring white terrycloth towels and white disposable towels and use both. Lay the terrycloth down first and the disposable towel over it. After each procedure, replace the disposable towel with a new one and put the soiled one in your trash container.

mini kit #5: wet manicuring supplies

☐ liquid soap to place in your finger bowl as a finger soak

☐ spray bottle of water labeled *water*

☐ finger bowl

☐ nylon manicure brush

Opening mini kit #5 should prompt you to:

1. Set out your spray bottle containing water. Disinfectant cannot touch the skin so you must rinse the disinfectant with water when removing the implements from the disinfectant container and dry them before use.

2. Place your finger bowl in the center of the table facing the model, and place the nail brush in between the finger bowl and yourself.

3. Set your antibacterial soap next to your finger bowl and nail brush.

mini kit #6: dry manicuring supplies

☐ cotton (must be in a dispenser or closed plastic bag)

☐ medium/fine abrasive board

☐ wooden pushers

☐ gloves (in case of an exposure incident)

Opening mini kit #6 should prompt you to:

1. Place your dispenser or bag of cotton on your table or in the drawer if available.

2. Place your abrasive board(s) on your table to the left.

3. Place your wooden pusher on your table.

mini kit #7: manicuring products

☐ hand lotion or massage cream

☐ cuticle remover

☐ cuticle oil

- [ ] nail oil

- [ ] red or designated color of nail polish

- [ ] topcoat

- [ ] base coat

- [ ] nail polish remover (if you are required to remove model's polish at the start of the manicure procedure)

- [ ] cotton-tipped wooden pusher (for cuticle care and removing excess polish from the fingers after your polish application)

- [ ] spatulas (for removing products from their container if this method is used or needed)

Opening Mini kit #7 should prompt you to:

1. Place all of your nail products/supplies in a neat and organized manner on your table. Polishes to your left and other products to your right.

Tech **Tip:**

This completes the manicure set up. You will most likely need to close your kit and keep it closed until directed to clean up and set your table for the next procedure.

nail tip exam

You will need the following products in addition to those already on your nail table from the initial table set up.

mini kit #8: nail tip application products

- [ ] box of assorted sized nail tips

- [ ] nail adhesive (bring extra just in case)

- [ ] medium abrasive boards (for blending the nail tip with the natural nail)

- [ ] buffer

- [ ] nylon manicure brush

- [ ] small bag labeled *trash* (replace the one attached to your table)

- [ ] small bag labeled *contaminated implements* (replace the one attached to your table)

- [ ] safety glasses or goggles (if required by your state) to use while applying adhesives

nail wrap exam

It is likely that you will have to demonstrate a nail wrap enhancement over the tip you applied during your practical exam.

 ## my state's requirements:

Check the material that you will be required to use.

- ☐ silk
- ☐ fiberglass
- ☐ linen
- ☐ paper

You will need the following products in addition to those already on your nail table from the initial table set up:

Tech **Tip:**

> Paper wraps are applied differently from other types of wraps, so if you are required to use paper wraps review the procedure with your instructor or trainer for directions.

mini kit #9: nail wrap application products

- ☐ Required nail wrap material
- ☐ Wrap resin
- ☐ Wrap resin accelerator (spray, mist, drop-on or brush-on)
- ☐ Nail oil (may be optional)
- ☐ fine abrasive board
- ☐ buffer
- ☐ new or disinfected nylon manicure brush

Tech **Tip:**

> Check if the material you use for your nail wrap demonstration can be precut, or if it must be in a strip or roll. You may need to cut your fabric during the exam, as part of your evaluation.

Tech **Tip:**

Sometimes nail oil is not allowed as it makes it difficult for the examiner to see the enhancement clearly. Check with your licensing division and your instructor about this.

monomer liquid and polymer powder nail examination

Most states require that you bring odorless nail products to your practical exam. This helps eliminate excessive odor in the examination room. Odorless monomer liquid and polymer powder products work differently than standard monomer liquid and polymer powder products. Therefore, you should practice with the exact odorless products that you will be required to use during your practical examination to familiarize yourself with how they work.

 my state's requirements:

Check which procedure you will be required to perform:

☐ One-color method

☐ Two-color method (French manicure look)

Which monomer liquid and polymer powder nail products are allowed? _____

_____

You will need the following products in addition to those already on your nail table from the initial table set up:

mini kit #10: odorless monomer liquid and polymer powder products

☐ cotton-tipped wooden pusher

☐ fine and medium abrasive boards

☐ nylon manicure brush

☐ buffer

☐ nail oil (may be optional)

☐ four dappen dishes (for your polymer powders, monomer liquid, and brush cleaner)

☐ small spoon or spatula (to remove the powder from your containers)

☐ polymer powder: white, pink or clear

- [ ] Application brushes

- [ ] brush cleaner

- [ ] odorless monomer liquid (must have the manufacturer's label)

- [ ] primer (must have the manufacturer's label)

- [ ] small 4x4 paper towels (to clean your brush in between bead placement)

- [ ] nail forms (take several disposable and reuasable just in case you need more than one)

- [ ] small bag labeled *trash* (replace the one attached to your table)

- [ ] small bag labeled *contaminated implements* (replace the one attached to your table)

- [ ] gloves and safety glasses/goggles (for the application of your nail primer)

Tech **Tip:**

Always remember to keep all products and jars capped when not in use. This will be included in your practical grade.

nail art

If you are required to perform flat nail art during your practical nail exam, you will want to follow the directions noted on your exam notice. The art is usually done on two nails and must be the same on both nails. Most states will require that it be flat nail art. Consult your instructor, trainer, or your admissions notice for the requirements for flat nail art.

You will be allotted a specific amount of time to complete your flat nail art application, therefore it is imperative that you practice your application until you have mastered it.

When deciding on the flat nail art design, it is a good idea to keep your design simple. This will allow you to perform the procedure with less difficulty and within the allotted time frame. Refer to your textbook for specific designs and techniques.

Tech **Tip:**

If you do not always have a model available, you should practice your selected flat nail art on nail tips to ensure that you are confident and comfortable with your selected design.

mini kit #11: nail art products

- [ ] _____
- [ ] _____
- [ ] _____
- [ ] _____
- [ ] _____
- [ ] _____
- [ ] _____

Chapter 24: Points To Remember

- [ ] All of the products you bring to your practical exam must have a manufacturer's label.

- [ ] All products that do not have a manufacturer's label, such as your water spray bottle, must be neatly hand-labeled.

- [ ] Check if your monomer and polymer nail products used during your practical exam need to be odorless.

- [ ] Find out if electricity is run to the exam tables and if you can bring a lamp.

- [ ] Be sure to include all documents needed as well as supplies in your kit.

Tech **Tip:**

If you still have questions about what products are allowed or what procedures to do when, write them down! Make a list of all your questions and put it in an envelope and tape it to your kit. That morning, quickly review your list to have it fresh in your mind. At the exam, ask the admissions person if there will be time for you to ask questions. Likely before the exam begins the examiners will brief you and give direction, this may be a time to get your questions answered. If not, raise your hand and ask! Better safe than sorry.

25

the day
of the exam

Congratulations, all your hard work has led you to this day. Don't worry, you've been trained well and you've practiced hard. It's time to prove to yourself and your examiners you know what you are doing! You are well dressed, feel confident, you have your kit and documents prepared and it's time to leave for the exam.

Now, let's do one final review to make sure you are ready!

Examination Day

Today you will most likely be taking both your written and your practical exam. Both will be timed, but you're prepared so you will do fine. Let's just do a final review to make sure you know exactly where you are going, and what to expect when you get there.

be on time

State boards are very strict about being on time. Being late may cause you to forfeit your testing time and date, so do not arrive late. Examiners will not allow you to enter the examination room after the practical exam has started.

Arrive at the examination site early. Most state examination sites require that you arrive 15 to 30 minutes before your scheduled testing time. Locate the building prior to your examination if you are not familiar with the examination location. This will help ensure that you arrive promptly. Anticipate delays and allow yourself plenty of time to arrive early, relax, collect your thoughts, and be ready to begin your examination. Anticipating delays will allow you time to handle any unforeseen circumstances.

my state's requirements:

Exam begins at: _____

Prior arrival time required by your state: _____

Examination site address: _____

Directions to site: _____

_____

travel

If you are required to travel some distance, it might be beneficial for you to spend the night at a hotel/motel the night before your scheduled examination date. By spending the night in a hotel/motel close to your examination site, you will allow yourself more time to rest, will be less stressed from driving, and will reduce your chances of being late. If you have arranged to share a room with your model or another student, keep in mind that you need adequate sleep and rest.

Hotel Reservations (if needed)

Hotel name: _____

Phone #: _____

Reservation confirmation #: _____

Room cost: $ _____

brain food

You should allow yourself extra time to eat breakfast on the morning of your examination. It is easier to concentrate on your examination when you are not concerned with fulfilling the basic human need of food. It is proven that you think better and quicker after you've eaten your first meal of the day.

before you leave for the exam checklist

- ☐ Had breakfast.
- ☐ Clothes are clean and professional.
- ☐ Shoes in good repair and clean/polished.
- ☐ You have your practical exam kit.
- ☐ All containers inside your kit have secured, leak-proof caps.
- ☐ Model's nails are prepared, and she has all required identification.
- ☐ Your required documentation and identification is in your kit.
- ☐ You have your admission notice.
- ☐ You have all equipment and materials that were too large to fit inside the kit.

Entering The Exam

You will not be admitted into the examination room without your required documentation. Make sure all of your required documentation is available and easy to access when you arrive at the examination site. Make sure you have an acceptable picture identification as some forms of picture identification are not considered official and will not be accepted.

If you are required to bring a model to your examination, make sure that your model has official picture identification as well.

follow directions

Once you're allowed into the exam site, listen carefully to all directions before setting up, and do not do anything until you are directed to do so.

Listening is an art. Because our minds have the ability to process words faster than we can speak them, we have a tendency to *hear* what someone is saying but not actually *listen* to what is being said. During the practical portion of the examination most participants are anxiously anticipating performing the procedures correctly, so you must take care to listen carefully to all directions. If the directions are not clear to you, raise your hand and ask the examiner to repeat.

Ask your model to follow your lead—she should listen to the directions being given, and she should follow any directions that pertain to her.

Rules At The Exam

Although requirements in each state are different, some rules will always apply.

talking to other participants during your examination

Talking to other participants or your model during your examination is prohibited. Some state examiners may ask you to leave the examination room if they see you talking. If this occurs, the examiners will neither ask for nor allow any explanation. This is not a school or salon where possibly talking your way out of a particular situation is an option. You will also want to turn off your cell phone and ask your model to do the same. You definitely do not want to talk on the phone on the exam floor or disturb others with your ring tone.

loaning or borrowing supplies and implements during your examination

You should not borrow or loan supplies or equipment to other participants during your examination. Being organized and prepared are part of following directions. If participants next to you begin talking or request to borrow supplies, simply ignore them. Do not jeopardize passing the examination by assisting another participant. Remind yourself of how long and hard you worked to ensure that you were ready and prepared. You are here for one reason: to pass your exam and become a licensed professional nail technician.

health and safety

During your practical examination, health and safety are a major consideration in your grading. Every procedure you are required to perform should be coupled with and emphasized by incorporating all health and safety requirements.

Purchase a small bottle of alcohol gel, antiseptic spray, and antiseptic hand wipes, or hand sanitizer. If permissible, leave the bottle on your table during your entire examination. You should always clean your hands and your model's hands before each specific procedure. This will assure the examiners that you know and follow all cleaning and disinfecting requirements.

In all probability your state will mandate that you bring a disinfectant. Make sure the container displays its original manufacturer's label. Use this disinfectant on your work area (table and chair/stools) before beginning your table set up. Keep your work area cleaned and disinfected throughout your practical examination.

After the completion of the examination, you should clean and disinfect your table, chair/stools, and surrounding work area again.

Be sure that you keep your work area (table), supplies, implements, and equipment in the most sanitary condition as possible before, during, and after your exam. Once an implement is used on any client, it is considered contaminated. To place a contaminated implement back onto your table causes your work area and supplies and implements to become contaminated. So be sure to put them in the bag labeled *contaminated implements* and not on your table.

Tips To Remember During The Exam

You have done all the preparation and practice, so now you can simply relax and perform what you know. Here are a few pointers to help keep you on track:

table setup

- Follow all directions explicitly, and do not start any procedure until directed to do so by the examiners. Do not attempt to perform more than what was directed. Do not look at or ask the participant next to you for guidance.

- As the examiners give you specific directions, you are expected to follow them verbatim—they expect no more and no less. The examiner may verbally state a specific set of directions such as, "begin your manicuring table setup." During their directions listen carefully and wait until they have been completed, then begin to perform the requested procedure.

- Do not begin any procedure or task before the directions are completed to be sure that you don't miss any vital information that may result in a mistake or misstep—in other words, you will not have followed directions. Being able to comprehend and follow directions is a crucial part of your practical examination.

manicure with massage and polish

If you have practiced and passed your "State Board Manicure Practice Exam" in chapter 13 of your workbook, you will have no problems passing it here at your state licensing examination. Take a deep breath, you will do fine. Here are a few tips to help ease your mind:

- Never apply massage cream directly to your model's skin; warm it in your hands first.

- Use smooth, rhythmic massage manipulations.

- Never break contact with your model's hands or arm during your manipulations.

- Thoroughly remove the massage cream from the nails after completing the massage movements.

- Upon completion of your polish application, make sure the polish is smooth, covers the entire nail plate, and that the skin, underside of the nail and eponychium are free from polish.

nail tip application

You will now apply a nail tip on the natural nail of your model's hand—you've done this hundreds of times by now, so this will be a piece of cake! Here are a few reminders, just in case:

- Make sure you perform all required nail prep procedures.

- Check that your nail tip properly fits your model's finger from sidewall to sidewall.

- Make sure you apply your safety glasses or goggles (if required by your state), and gloves when using an adhesive.

- Remember when blending the nail tip flush to the natural nail to keep the file flat on the nail to avoid damaging the natural nail and making grooves in the nail.

- Hold the sidewalls when filing.

- Take care not damage the cuticle area when filing the nail.

- Don't forget to incorporate the Stop, Rock, and Hold Procedures:

1. You can feel the **stop** when the tip rests against the free edge of the natural nail. You should be holding the nail tip at a 45-degree angle.

2. **Rock** the nail tip onto the natural nail plate. This helps eliminate air bubbles.

3. **Hold** the nail tip in place on the natural nail until it dries. This usually takes about 10 seconds.

4. Apply another drop or bead of adhesive/adhesive to the seam between the natural nail and the nail tip. This anchors the tip to the natural nail more securely.

nail wrap enhancement

If you have practiced and passed your "State Board Tip and Wrap Practice Exam" in chapter 16 of your workbook, you will have no problems passing it today at your state licensing examination. Relax you know this, and here are a few tips that may help:

- Cleanse your hands and your model's hand and fingers.

- Make sure you wear your safety glasses or goggles (if required by your state) when applying adhesive and wrap resins.

- Cut fabric to the width and shape of the nail plate.

- Trim the fabric to fit 1/16 inch away from the sides and free edge.

- Be careful not to allow the adhesive to get on the cuticle area or in the sidewalls of the nail.

- Do not buff too hard as you can buff through the material.

monomer liquid and polymer powder enhancement

You have practiced this technique with odorless products for months and passed your "State Board Monomer Liquid and Polymer Powder Practice Exam" in chapter 17 of your workbook. You will have no problems passing this today at your state licensing examination. Relax, you know this, and here are a few tips to refresh your memory:

- Wear gloves and safety glasses or goggles (if required by your state) when applying primer.

- Allow the primer to dry naturally. Do not attempt to hasten its drying time by fanning the nail with your hands or other objects.

- Take care when filing the nail enhancement so you do not damage the surrounding skin.

- Make sure your nail enhancement is smooth, even, and not too thick.

- Observe your completed nail shape by holding it out in front of you at eye level with the free edge facing you. Make sure your nail has a consistent shape, thickness, and is free from dips, splits, or cracks.

final clean up checklist

At the conclusion of your practical exam, you should gather all supplies, implements, and equipment and place them in your kit. Don't forget your *trash* and *contaminated implement* bags. Many state practical exams incorporate your final cleanup as part of your exam grade, so make sure that you leave everything clean and neat.

After you have gathered all of your personal belongings, you should check to ensure you have completely cleaned your work area:

☐ Clean and disinfect your table.

☐ Clean and disinfect the drawer if there is one present at your table.

☐ Clean and disinfect your model's chair/stool.

☐ Clean and disinfect your chair/stool.

☐ Pick up any trash or supplies that may have fallen on the floor.

☐ Push in either chairs or stools so they are in alignment with the table.

Chapter 25: Points To Remember

☐ You will not be allowed into the exam without the proper documents and identification.

☐ You must be on time or early for your exam.

☐ You will be allotted a specific amount of time to complete each procedure.

☐ Always work with clean and disinfected tools, implements, and supplies.

☐ If you have a drawer in your manicuring table, clean and disinfect it before beginning your exam.

☐ Keep your work area clean and neat at all times.

☐ Safety and sanitation will be graded throughout your entire examination.

☐ Clean and disinfect your work area (table) and chairs/stools before and after your exam.

☐ If your kit is used as a dry sanitizer, it must remain closed during your examination. You may only open it during table set-up for each procedure.

You're Done!

Congratulations on your new career in nail technology! It will be a fun, exciting, and lucrative life experience. Enjoy your new career and never stop learning.

Notes

Notes

Notes

Notes

Notes

Notes

Notes

Notes

Notes